The Effective Leader

Rupert Eales-White

KOGAN PAGE | *CREATING SUCCESS*

First published in Great Britain in 2003

Kogan Page Limited
120 Pentonville Road
London N1 9JN
United Kingdom
www.kogan-page.co.uk

British Library Cataloguing in Publication Data

A CIP record for this book is available from the British Library.

ISBN 0 7494 3913 0

Typeset by Jean Cussons Typesetting, Diss, Norfolk
Printed and bound in Great Britain by Clays Ltd, St Ives plc

contents

introduction

This book will enable you to become an effective leader in today's work environments of change and learning. Not only will you realise that you have, at this moment of reading, the potential to be world-class in your leadership, but you will be provided with the detail of what is required and how to achieve what is required. Additionally, you will learn practical tools, techniques, skills and behaviours that will guarantee your success as an effective leader.

In the first chapter, we look at how words like 'boss' and 'subordinate' can lead us subconsciously into inappropriate leadership behaviours, and how we need to see ourselves, when in the leadership role, as 'creators of growth and learning' in ourselves and in those we lead. This attitude and corresponding actions will optimise our own performance in the work place as well as the performance of those we lead. The chapter concludes by putting our leadership into the context of all the other roles we carry out on a daily basis, when at work.

The second chapter, 'Defining effective leadership', asks you to develop a template of both ineffective and effective leadership, based on your own experience as a follower. We then share the views of a group of senior managers running a Malaysian multinational company, and distil a template of effective leadership derived from the views of over 1000 managers and leaders operating in different countries and different cultures. The key message is that you can be an effective leader by simply carrying out the actions required – there is no need for charisma. However, ineffective leadership also lurks within us, and the behaviours of ineffective leaders are set out and those highlighted that must be avoided at all costs. Otherwise we will destroy the trust of those we lead. Trust once gone takes an age to return.

The third chapter, 'Creating growth for yourself', focuses on you the individual: how to build your self-confidence, develop awareness, overcome limiting beliefs, structure your thinking and improve your performance. You will not be able to create growth for others until you have learnt how to create growth for yourself.

In the next chapter, we ask you to complete a questionnaire to determine your perception of your leadership orientation, and obtain a trusted 'other' to determine their perception of your leadership orientation. We look at the nature of perception gaps, how they arise and how they can be overcome, as well as considering your leadership style and examining how developing flexibility in style – being able to choose the right style to suit the situation you face or the competence of your follower – enables you to become much more effective.

In Chapter 5, 'Developing core leadership skills', we cover the two core practical skills you will need on your voyage of discovery: questioning and listening.

Chapter 6, 'Improving staff performance', looks at how to develop clarity of role, set standards and performance measures, give praise and constructive criticism, coach and mentor, use appraisals to create learning and growth, and motivate your staff.

Chapter 7 sets out all the key skills, techniques and processes required to build effective teams, one of the key requirements of today's leaders. The effective team is not only the most efficient way of operating in the workplace but also the most effective way to accelerate individual learning. Effective team working also eliminates the negative aspects of corporate culture and office politics.

The final chapter 'Leading change', looks at how you reacted to a sudden change in the past, perceived negatively, and from those reactions we distil what is termed the reaction or transition curve. We then consider how you can progress through the curve, and how you can ensure that those you lead progress. We look at behaviours in key stages, and what strategies are required to lead your staff from initial denial to complete commitment. We conclude this chapter by asking you to complete the change preference questionnaire, then consider what it means and how you can gain personal benefit from change.

putting your leadership role in context

In this first chapter, we look at our instinctive definition of leadership, and then put leadership into its context – the roles we carry out in the workplace.

how we instinctively define leadership

Our instinctive definition of leadership can be summarised by one word that is common to all cultures and languages I have encountered. The word is 'boss'. To boss about or around means, according to the *Concise Oxford Dictionary*, 'to be domineering or overbearing towards (others)'. Of course, we don't actually go around behaving like that to those we lead. However, I have heard many instances of bosses who, when under severe stress (and sometimes when not under any stress at all!), are domineering towards those they lead. When we are under stress we tend to revert to our instinctive view of leader-ship, 'I am the boss.'

---

case history

In the 1990s, a colleague and I were running a week-long senior management development programme for a very large company, mainly operating out of its domestic market. (The location of the country is irrelevant, as I have heard a number of such stories in many countries and across many cultures.) The ablest delegate was the chief executive officer (CEO) of a subsidiary whose turnover was around a billion pounds. He was also the most like-able delegate, and we had a few private chats after the formal evening meal. He was very stressed, which was not surprising as he had considerable responsibility and worked very hard – around 80 hours a week, Mondays to Saturdays, week in week out. What caused him the greatest stress is what happened on his day off, where he wanted to relax and unwind with his wife and young family. Every Sunday, without fail, he was summoned to his boss's home to be screamed at for an hour before being sent back to his own home.

Language does not help, with the definition of those we lead as our 'subordinates'. The dictionary comes through with 'of lesser order or importance' and 'under the authority and control of another'. Of course, if we think of those we lead as of lesser order and importance than us and under our authority and control, we will, when under stress, 'boss' them around. Fortunately the word 'subordinate', though still commonplace, is being replaced by follower, direct report or team member.

However, we still have a problem if the words we use inter-nally – our self-talk – are 'leader' and 'follower'. 'Leader' is defined as 'a person who rules or guides others' and 'follower' as 'a person who accepts the teachings of another'. We cannot change the words that are in such common usage, but we can change how we subconsciously think about leadership, if we are prepared to change our concept. This can be achieved by repeating every day many times to ourselves. 'I am a COGAL, I am a COGAL'. If we repeat that sufficiently often, then we will change our instinctive definition of leadership from 'boss' or 'leader' to COGAL.

What on earth, you are asking, is a COGAL? Leaders of today should see their primary function as creators of growth and learning (COGAL) in themselves and in those for whom they are responsible. The result will be that the performance of the leaders and those they lead will be optimised, which means they provide maximum benefits to the organisations and clients they serve.

our work roles

Figure 1.1, a development of a model created by Professor Drucker, sets out the key work roles we carry out each day of our working lives. Any manager carries out five roles, and it is helpful to put work activities and skills deployed into a role context. By explicitly recognising what role we are carrying out at any given moment in time, we know what particular skill set we should be using, and therefore carry out the role more effectively than if we simply dipped into a generic tool bag to carry out all our work activities. I will examine briefly each role, before making some general points.

The five core work roles identified are leadership, followership, client, technical, and administration. We will look at each in turn.

leadership

This book concentrates on how we can be effective in the leadership role. Whether supervisor, junior manager, departmental

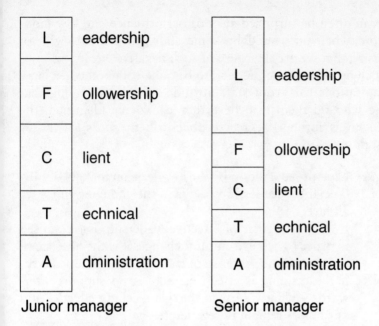

Figure 1.1 *Roles and mix (Drucker, 1967)*

manager, senior manager or executive, we have a responsibility and a duty to lead those we are put in charge of as effectively as we possibly can. We will be exploring the nature of the leadership role in depth from a practical and action-oriented perspective. However, for many in a leadership role – and that role starts as soon as we are put in a position of authority over another member of staff – there is no exploration, because there is no explicit recognition of the role.

For those of us who do not consciously think of ourselves as leaders (or COGALs!) and so cannot plan to act effectively whenever we carry out the role, necessarily we tend to focus on the job or ourselves and not our followers. Nevertheless we provide subconsciously, without thought or control, a pattern of behaviour and approach that sets boundaries on the motivation and performance of those we are not consciously leading.

We can often be surprised at poor performance and low motivation (when uncovered by some staff attitude survey), not
realising that we are the cause of such negative effects.

Such negative outcomes tend to be quite common when large
organisations carry out staff attitude surveys, assuming that
those who fill them in believe they cannot be identified (the
same holds for 360-degree feedback on the boss). The key
reasons are:

▓ Lack of recognition by the key decision makers of how
   crucial the leadership role is in the changing times we
   all face.
▓ If the importance of effective leadership is recognised
   in order to achieve cultural change, it is the absence of
   training or the presence of training that is ineffective.
▓ If the training is effective, there is no support afterwards – what is termed the 'glass ceiling effect' – and
   our bosses remain unregenerate.

On an optimistic note, we have enormous power as leaders to
create – through the deployment of effective approaches, attitudes, and skills – subcultures that transform the competence
and motivation of our followers, irrelevant of the cultural
norms in the company/our own boss's leadership style.

We are in a leadership role whenever we communicate with a
'subordinate', whether electronically, by telephone, in one-to-
one meetings or 'team' meetings. If you were to carry out a
time-and-motion study you would find that you spend a lot of
the working day in this vital role – likely to be much more than
any initial estimate.

followership

We are also followers or in a 'subordinate' role. I will use that
pejorative term as well as the term 'boss' as the words are so
prevalent across so many countries and cultures.

If leadership training is scarce, then followership training is non-existent. We learn how to be a follower by absorbing the culture and modifying our behaviour, depending on our understanding, interest and political skill, according to the unwritten rules we pick up along the way. As Robert E Kelley said, 'Followership is not a person but a role, and what distinguishes followers from leaders is not intelligence nor character, but the role they play. Effective followers and effective leaders are often the same people playing different parts at different hours of the day.'

For those of you interested in considering the follower role in more depth (and how effective we are can determine whether we are promoted ahead of the pack or escape the next 'downsizing'), I would refer you to his excellent *Harvard Review Business* article (see 'references and further reading').

We carry out the followership role whenever we interact with our boss or bosses (if we are in a matrix structure) or more senior staff, whenever we attend a meeting as a team member, and so on.

client

This role was not part of Professor Drucker's original model. Today, we all have external or internal clients. We put our 'client hat' on whenever we interact with our internal/external clients – whether by letter/fax/e-mail, telephone or meeting. The core skills required to be effective in this role are relationship management skills, many of which will be covered when looking in depth at how we can be more effective leaders

technical

The technical role is our business role, when we carry out activities that define our professional competence, as lawyer, architect, consultant, product manager, production supervisor, salesperson, strategic planner, business development manager, administrator, IT manager, and so on. The combination of focus on the technical and client roles and absence of training in the leadership role explains why so many managers are poor delegators, and work very long hours to less than optimum effect

administration

The final role is self-explanatory. Our working lives are full of administrative matters. We have to organise ourselves, and deal with the large volumes of paper and electronic information that result from being part of an organisation.

The five core roles define any managerial job. However, the role mix varies depending on the job itself. A research scientist would have a very large technical role, a managing director a very large leadership role.

As suggested, it is very helpful to think in terms of such roles, all of which we are likely to carry out more than once in a working day. The two key reasons are these.

First, we can identify the skills requirement of each role, the degree of overlap and degree of separation. We can devise and implement a plan to maximise our competence in each role. The lack of separation into roles has reduced the perception of importance of the 'soft' roles of leadership and followership and over-emphasised the importance of the 'hard' roles of technical and administration – with a severe reduction in personal and corporate effectiveness as a result. When did you last produce, never mind update, your action plan to be an effective follower and leader? I have little doubt that you have, and review regularly, an action plan to meet your business targets.

Second, we can identify which work activity slots into which role, and therefore apply the appropriate skill or competence to that activity. It is a good idea to develop a role mind-set, to

recognise when we are switching roles and what is the appropriate mind-set for that role. Often we can leave a meeting as a
follower or with our 'client' hat on, feeling frustrated or angry,
and without pausing for thought vent our anger on a subordinate, only to regret it afterwards and apologise. If we
consciously recognised the switch in roles, we would have
tempered our approach to our own follower and been a more
effective leader as a result.

Having looked at our subconscious views of leadership and
the need to think COGAL, and examined the context in which
we carry out our leadership role, we now turn to determining a
practical and detailed definition of what effective leaders do
and how they do it.

defining effective leadership

Now we have put leadership into its context, let us consider the detail of what constitutes effective leadership. We are going to look at this from three perspectives: the followers' view of effective leadership, the followers' view of ineffective leadership and the leaders' view of effective leadership.

followers' view of effective leadership

I want you to get a pencil and paper, pause for a few minutes and consider your own personal experience of leadership, thinking of specific individuals in your life for whom you have been in the 'followership' role. You do not need to make it work-specific, but think of all those individuals: parents, teachers, 'gang' leaders, lecturers and your bosses since entering work. Think back and think of any actions these individuals took that you felt motivated you and helped. List all the different actions, focusing only on what was positive for you.

I do not know what you have written, but I have asked this question of many groups of managers from many companies and different cultures. It is surprising just how much commonality of thought from personal experience emerges. To start with, I will share the views of a group of senior managers and executives of a Malaysian multinational. Figure 2.1 sets out the list, then we summarise the discussion that took place under each item on the list.

▓ Think explicitly about their leadership role.
▓ Develop awareness and self-belief.
▓ Focus externally – listen, support, provide feedback and coach.
▓ Display integrity in decision taking and take decisions.
▓ Share information.
▓ Be confident enough to make mistakes, admit mistakes and learn from mistakes.
▓ Direct with coaching.
▓ Delegate authority as well as responsibility.

Figure 2.1 *Malaysian multinational managers' views of effective leaders*

think explicitly about their leadership role

One of the reasons identified for poor leadership was thoughtlessness. It was recognised that abruptness or inadequate briefings, or being left to twiddle your thumbs while your boss chatted on the telephone, was rarely a deliberate insult, nor did it mean that the subordinate was held in low esteem. It was simply the result of thoughtlessness.

As mentioned in the previous chapter, we do not spend much, if any, time explicitly thinking about ourselves as leaders or COGALs. We may wrestle with a complex technical or task issue, plan to deal with an awkward client, prepare a presentation, think long and hard about a report we are writing and how we are going to sell it, but we spend little time thinking about the leadership role that we perform much of the time.

Effective leaders think about their leadership role and plan their leadership strategy in much the same way as they do for all these other important matters.

develop awareness and self-belief

Ineffective leaders display an excess of control, usually because they either need to control or want to control. The Malaysian managers' debate in this instance focused on need, which was perceived as arising fundamentally from uncertainty. The identified sources of uncertainty were the individuals themselves and/or changes in the business environment. A lack of security and self-belief could be subconscious, and therefore difficult to deal with because of a lack of recognition.

Effective leaders developed an awareness of self. They identified, acknowledged and understood their strengths and weaknesses, believed in themselves and their competence and capability. Leaders had to think positively about themselves before they could think positively about those they led. The more they were in control of themselves, the less they needed to control others.

focus externally: listen, support, provide feedback and coach

Ineffective leaders focus on themselves. By developing self-awareness, and by becoming comfortable with themselves, effective leaders can do what those being led want: focus on the follower.

Effective leaders were good listeners, providing support at both the logical and emotional levels, and providing feedback to encourage their followers and enable them to develop.

Additionally, effective leaders were good coaches: they asked the awkward questions (in an empathetic way) that enabled followers to discover and learn for themselves, rather than be told what to do. Both these are key elements of the leader as COGAL.

display integrity in decision taking and take decisions

Some ineffective leaders took bad and inconsistent decisions to accommodate the changing power shifts in the body politic or the changing views of those in command. Others took no decisions and delegated them by default, to avoid offending anyone adversely affected by the decision.

share information

Jan Carlson of Scandinavian Airlines made the remark that, 'An individual without information cannot take responsibility; an individual with information cannot help but take responsibility.' Effective leaders recognised that their followers wanted responsibility and so shared information. They operated a 'need to know' policy from the follower and not the organisational perspective.

be confident enough to make mistakes, admit mistakes and learn from mistakes

Ineffective leaders denied learning and effective problem solving to themselves and their followers because they needed to be perceived as infallible. The word 'confidence' was first used here. That is the outcome of self-awareness and self-belief, allied with the humility to recognise that capability does not mean infallibility, and that change requires continuous learning.

direct with coaching

This point recognised that there are occasions when any junior executive/manager or staff member needs direction or guidance, especially when in an unfamiliar role or handling a new task beyond his or her current capability. The 'with coaching' part reflected the approach required, when the leader was in a necessary control mode.

delegate authority as well as responsibility

This was a particular issue with this culture, but it occurs elsewhere, and strikes at the heart of effective leadership – knowing when to hand over the reins, as well as the horse!

Before looking at a model of effective leadership, it is worth sharing the research finding from a survey by Management Centre Europe, on what more than 1000 European managers considered the attributes of a successful business leader, and whether their own managing director had the desired attributes. I have limited the results to those where the desired attribute was mentioned by more than three-quarters of the respondents, so as to focus on the priorities.

		Desired %	Actual %
1.	Able to build effective teams	96	50
2.	Knows how to listen	93	44
3.	Capable of making decisions on his own	87	66
4.	Knows how to retain good people	86	39
5.	Surrounds himself with the top people	85	50
6.	Energetic	85	62
7.	Innovative	83	47
8.	Visionary	79	45
9.	Has high ethical standards	76	53

Figure 2.2 *Key attributes of a successful business leader (Eales-White, 1992)*

It is fascinating to note the desire for an externally focused leader, and that the biggest gap is in 'knows how to listen'. We look at listening skills in Chapter 4.

Finally, I draw your attention to Figure 2.3. Key points are:

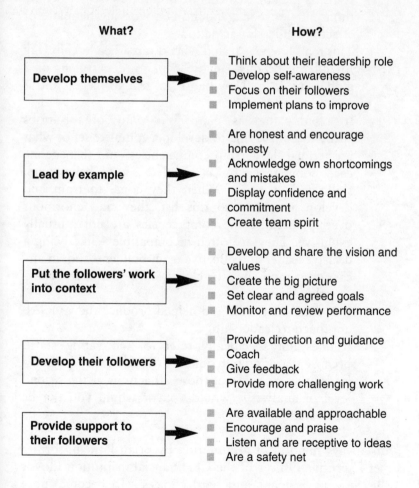

Figure 2.3 *The effective leader*

■ This approach is in accordance with the principles of structured thinking. Structured thinking forges the link between the strategic and the detail, and enables the individual to think and write in a persuasive and logical way. It is covered in Chapter 4.

■ It distils the key elements of all the views expressed by thousands of managers and is a working template of effective leadership in action.

■ This template was tested when I ran a Leadership Day for all the partners in the banking department of a global law firm. They had it to 'tear to pieces' and it proved to be robust.

■ It avoids 'analysis paralysis'. Many organisations spend months trying to develop a complete set of what are termed 'leadership competencies' and then define each competence by a complete set of behaviours, skills and attitudes. When they come to train and develop according to this list, they find enormous overlap, because the competencies are not mutually exclusive. They are often incompatible – like being a decisive leader and effective team-builder – and, in any case, it is impossible to achieve all these desired behavioural outcomes

■ It is consistent with and helped produce the COGAL approach to leadership.

■ It does not specifically refer to 'motivating staff', because that is an outcome. If you, as a follower, had a leader that carried out those 20 actions at the second level of analysis – would you or would you not be motivated?

I am always mindful of a quotation by Brian Pitman, former Chief Executive Officer of the UK financial institution Lloyds TSB: 'Strategy is focus and hard choices'. To become more effective leaders, we need to select key action areas and then focus on making them happen.

Looking at your own list and the list of 20 actions, I ask you the key question I pose to all the managers who produced the list. Which of the actions do you feel you could not now do or learn how to do? When I ask this question, invariably all the managers say, 'At a pinch, we could do them all, or learn how to do them.'

This leads to a fundamental conclusion about you and leadership. We can all be effective leaders. 'Actions speak louder than words.' If we do the right things at the right time in the right way, we will all be brilliant leaders. We can become leaders, and do not have to be born leaders. The model of heroic leadership – the Charge of the Light Brigade – is or should be long dead. Nor need we be charismatic.

followers' view of ineffective leadership

I would ask you to repeat the previous exercise, but this time focus on everything that demotivated you, upset or annoyed you. Accentuate the negative from past experience. Again, I do not know your list (and we have had some aspects of ineffective leadership in the Malaysian multinational example), but this is one list that a group of managers produced. Ineffective (or bad) leaders:

- did not listen;
- failed to delegate or simply dumped;
- showed no interest in you;
- did not respect you;
- gave negative feedback to a third party;
- did not give praise when praise was due;
- criticised you in front of others;
- took personal credit for your ideas;
- were always taking control;
- bullied you;

- ▓ did not give you the tools to do the job;
- ▓ did not keep you informed;
- ▓ did not set clear objectives;
- ▓ showed favouritism – one rule for one, another for others;
- ▓ were intransigent and closed-minded.

Interestingly, when asked the question; 'which of these actions (in a worst-case scenario, and having crossed your heart to tell the whole truth and nothing but the truth) would you not be capable of committing?', what do think was the reply? You have got it. The good and the bad leader is one and the same person – you or I. As Thomas Carlisle said, 'The ideal is in thyself, the impediment is in thyself also.'

So it is a question not of becoming an effective leader by trying to follow some externally developed prescription, but of discovering the effective leader in yourself. What you can achieve is continuous improvement, more and more occasions when you act as an effective leader, and fewer and fewer when you act in the opposite direction. This leads need to another fundamental truth.

You should aim to be a 70 per cent leader.

Let me give an example of exactly what I mean. A most competent woman – we will call her Julie – decided that, in her early 40s, she had one more big job in her. She moved within her sector into a senior management role with one of the blue-chip players. She had been a client, and I had a couple of lunches with her in the first six months of her new job. She was fairly demotivated at the first lunch, and more so at the second. So I introduced the 70 per cent rule, in this case applied to job satisfaction. The four key points I made were:

- ▓ Never aim for 100 per cent. Life is not like that, because we are human and not divine. Moreover, if we aim for the impossible, we are guaranteed dissatisfaction and to fail. (The three key areas where we should never aim for 100 per cent are job satisfaction, key relationships such as partner or parent, and leadership, whenever we have a leadership role.) Many, many people spend their lives with a ratio of less than 50/50, and the higher the expectations given to young people, the more dissatisfied they will become as a result.

▓ The aim should be 70 per cent. (For fans of Sherlock Holmes – the 70 per cent solution.)

▓ She should look at her current situation and determine the current percentage split (for example, 70/30 meaning 70 per cent of the time she was enjoying her work and 30 per cent she was not).

▓ If the current percentage was not 70/30 but nearer 50/50, then she should develop and implement plans to move to the required ratio.

▓ If the percentage split was very unfavourable, perhaps 30/70, then she should implement a short-term rescue operation to get to 50/50, and if that failed, leave.

Julie agreed with all this, and we looked at her current situation. The core positives were:

▓ a challenging, interesting job;
▓ very bright, intelligent and able colleagues.

The core negatives were:

▓ lack of clarity in her role;
▓ a boss who was fine at the personal relationship level, but too demanding and controlling at the work level;
▓ insufficient resources to carry out her role;
▓ too much overseas travel.

She estimated the percentage split at 30/70, so we developed a rescue plan to bring her to 50/50, focusing on her getting clarity in her work role. The chosen approach was for Julie to draft and suggest to her boss a job description, focused on how she could provide him with maximum support and enhance his ability to do his own job, and so motivate him to use all his greater political power to make it happen.

Let us now look at how the 70 per cent rule applies to becoming an effective leader. At the moment most of you reading this book will be around 50/50 in carrying out the actions of effective leaders, though some will be nearer 40/60 and others 60/40. This is because you will have been in a situation of 'I don't know I don't know' – not aware of what it takes to be effective. So you will, on average, be in a 50/50 position. On the actions that ineffective leaders take, you will (as a human being, and being stressed at times) again on average be in a 50/50 position.

You can move towards say 80 or 90 per cent progressively over time on the effective actions (in a focused and structured way – see Chapter 3), and reduce your use of the ineffective actions progressively over time, towards 10–20 per cent. This will bring you to the (approximately) 70 per cent solution.

Finally, you can never eliminate the negatives, but it is a very good idea to look at the list to uncover the ineffective actions you know you are capable of and have carried out in the past. I encourage all the managers I train in effective leadership to do this. Then you can pick the few you consider must be eliminated. The criteria for selection is simple. 'If I indulge in these, I will destroy the trust I must develop or have with my followers.' Trust once destroyed takes an age to recreate, and means that you have destroyed any chance of becoming an effective leader in the short to medium term.

leaders' view of effective leadership

I will not ask you to put on your leadership hat now and write down all the actions you should take to be an effective leader, for two reasons. First, your opinions will now be coloured by reading this chapter. Second, when I have asked groups of managers to go into syndicate rooms to consider this question, their conclusions mirror very closely the conclusions of the follower group sharing their experience of effective leadership.

In the next chapter we look at those aspects not yet covered of developing or growing yourself, a process that is necessary before you can develop your followers.

creating growth for yourself

In this chapter we look at how you can grow, which is necessary before you can help other people grow. Specifically we look at how you can build your self-confidence, develop awareness, overcome limiting beliefs, structure your thinking and improve your performance.

building self-confidence

I will focus on two powerful techniques, both of which will help you build your self-confidence and enable you to face any situation in the future. They are creating affirmative statements, and building a ring of confidence

creating affirmative statements

Look back on your past and think of, and write down, all your successes – any achievements you feel proud of. There is no maximum, but you should continue until you have at least 10.

Take the achievement of which you are most proud, and answer the question, 'What are all the skills and qualities I demonstrated to achieve this success?' Continue to ask the same question about your other successes, until you have a list of at least 20 different skills/qualities. If one of your qualities is not persistence, then please persist. It is very, very motivational to spend as much time as it takes to drag out all these skills and qualities, which we all possess, as we all have successes, however small we may think them.

Next develop three affirmative statements, each with three related qualities and skills. For example:

▓ I focus on clients, am a good listener and develop rapport easily.
▓ I am hard working, well organised and disciplined.
▓ I am friendly, supportive and generous.

These are generic statements that are true for you (not a 'wish' or 'will' list). You should memorise them and use them whenever you feel the need. It is often quite helpful to start the day with them, putting you into a confident and positive frame of mind.

An important point is that different people have different ways of processing information. The three primary ways are auditory, visual and kinaesthetic (feelings-based). While we can use all three, we often prefer one to another. You should use all three to have the greatest impact: memorise the list, create a picture of yourself behaving as indicated by each affirmative statement (which is why I suggested they be connected), and generate positive attitudes and emotions.

Additionally, when you know you have a particular change to make or project to complete, you can develop affirmative statements that are specific to the requirements for success in the future. Look back to the pool of qualities and skills you have developed, choose those needed, and write specific affirmative statements. Again picture success and create the positive feelings associated with success.

building a ring of confidence

1. Think back to a situation where you felt on the top of the world, and fully confident.
2. Recall all the positive emotions you had, using all the ways to process information – visual, auditory and kinaesthetic.
3. Recreate the same emotional state.
4. Draw an (imaginary) circle in the ground in front of you, and when and only when you are in that positive state, step into the circle. This is the ring of confidence.
5. Step out when you want to come back down to earth. Repeat twice, and when you step out for the last time, try not to let go.

Again, whenever you are facing a situation that holds some concerns for you, you can use this technique to build your confidence.

developing awareness

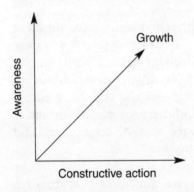

Figure 3.1 *Developing awareness*

This is a very powerful and simple model. It applies at all levels: organisational, departmental, team and individual.

What the model says is that we have to develop our awareness and take constructive action in order to grow. It is not sufficient to develop our awareness of self, of others, of life, of everything, if we continue to act as if we are not aware. An example might be someone who has read widely and deeply and developed knowledge, understanding and awareness, but all this has stayed in the world of books, and the person has continued to live life unaffected by it.

It is not sufficient to act in a positive and constructive way, to do the right things, if we are not aware why those actions are helpful. Clearly if we are the kind of person who tends to be positive and take constructive action, that gives us a head start in terms of our current level of growth. However, without being aware, we cannot direct the path of action or continue to grow. So we need to make a conscious link between the two, to apply our enhanced awareness to be more constructive in what we do.

Here are some specific strategies that will enable us to develop our awareness:

- Dedicate quality time to raising awareness.
- Become as little children again. When we were young, we asked many, many 'whats', 'whys' and 'hows' (see next chapter on questioning) which enabled us to learn.
- Specifically uncover and challenge the implicit assumptions that underpin our thinking and beliefs. This will enable us to accept more readily new ideas that do not fit with our existing thinking.
- Learn to listen to the messages we receive and not be distracted by who the messenger is and how the message is conveyed.
- Notice and control our tendency to 'justify': to answer unasked questions, 'explain' our weaknesses, defend ourselves unnecessarily.
- Develop a positive attitude to ourselves and others. The glass is always half full.

You will be able to develop your awareness in Chapter 5, assuming you fill in the questionnaire on your leadership orientation, and in Chapter 8, assuming you complete the change preference questionnaire,

overcoming limiting beliefs

We all develop beliefs that limit our scope for action and our ability to grow and achieve.

example

Have you ever heard of an athlete called Cliff Young? He was an unknown 61-year-old farm worker who entered the long-distance Melbourne-Sydney race. He had little idea of what was a good or bad time. He won the race, beating some of the world's greatest athletes, by one and a half days. He had none of the conventional wisdom or limiting beliefs that held back his fellow competitors. Sometimes ignorance is bliss.

We can compare Cliff Young's and the other athletes' beliefs.

Table 3.1

Other athletes	Cliff Young
Special training was needed	Practice was running around a sheep station
Special equipment was needed	Overalls and boots should be worn
The race should be run like a marathon	You should shuffle along (later this was found to be the most efficient way to run very long distances)
The pattern should be run 18 hours, sleep 6 hours	Cliff didn't know that sleep was allowed

We think and behave in a way consistent with our beliefs. When there is a mismatch between our beliefs and our results, our thinking and behaviour 'automatically' change so as to make our results consistent with our beliefs. So if you identify the beliefs that limit development and growth, that can be the starting point to improving your performance.

At the time of writing this book, I am in the middle of doing a diploma in performance coaching, as I like to tackle at least one major area for new learning each year. Seeking inspiration as to how these limiting beliefs are uncovered, I looked at the relevant section of the text – to discover they suggested I listed my strengths and weaknesses. I then tried a frontal approach and asked my wife to set out all her beliefs. Naturally, she only mentioned positive beliefs. Limiting beliefs are held in the subconscious, and some are difficult to recognise, as they are negative, even prejudicial. Eventually, I struck gold and found a method that worked. I would like you to do the following.

step 1

Write down everything you believe you are not good at. Funnily enough, that won't be too difficult. Most managers I have worked with find it easy to identify the things they think they do badly, and often difficult to identify the things they do well. The reason, I believe, is that too many people in this world think the glass is half empty, rather than half full. As a result, once we are no longer young children (and for some, even when we are) we tend to receive frequent criticism of our weaknesses and rare praise of our strengths.

step 2

For each item on the list, putting on as objective a hat as you possibly can, think why you believe you do this badly. You may have to be very tough on yourself and keep persisting for each item. For a given reason, that might be an effect and not the fundamental cause. Keep asking why until you have hit rock bottom. Then you will have found what you can work on to overcome the limiting belief.

step 3

Develop a plan to eradicate the cause and hence overcome the limiting belief. Remember we all have the potential to improve, and the power of positive thinking to produce positive action.

Let us take an example.

I am useless at presentations.
> *So why do you think so?*
> Because the only time I have ever made a presentation I was useless.
> *What do you think caused that poor performance?*
> I was a bag of nerves. I lost my thread at the start and never recovered.
> *Why do you think you were so nervous?*
> I just lacked confidence. I was familiar with the material – learnt it by heart – but I found having a big audience so intimidating, I cracked up.
> *What do you think would help you to give a fantastic presentation?*
> I suppose if I learnt all the tricks and techniques beforehand and rehearsed till I got it right, I would be more confident and might do a bit better.
> *You will do fantastically. You just need to go on that excellent presentation skills course run at Sefton.*

Note: Whilst you can be your own questioner, if you have a trusted friend/colleague or partner, using him or her will be beneficial. This person would be acting as your coach, rather than you coaching yourself, which can be tougher.

structuring your thinking

There is a powerful and simple methodology to improve both our thinking and written communication, enabling us to link high-level concepts (strategy) to detail, and move from the detail to the high level, and create a compelling written argument with impeccable logic. We will take the core leadership model as an example. The structure is as follows

1. Describe the **situation** or context. This is background to the thinking or writing. In our case the situation is that *we are in a leadership role.*
2. Introduce a **complication** or reason to write or think: *we could be more effective in our leadership role.*
3. Decide on the **key question** that naturally arises in the reader's (thinker's) mind as a result of the complication: *what are we going to do about this?*
4. Resolve this question by producing the **governing thought** or high-level answer that drives the rest of the thinking: *we become effective leaders.*
5. Determine the generic question that drives the answers at the **keyline**: *what do effective leaders do?*
6. Produce the **answers**:
   - Develop themselves.
   - Put work into context.
   - Develop their followers.
   - Lead by example.
   - Support their followers.
7. For each of the answers, determine the question that naturally flows into the reader's/thinker's mind, then produce the **answers at the next level**. Here there is another generic question 'How?', but you can have different questions at this level.

For example:

Situation: I am attending a presentation skills course.
Complication: I need to prepare a five-minute presentation on a topic I find interesting.
Key question: What shall I talk about?

Governing thought: I will share my experiences of my holiday in South Africa.
Question: Where will I focus my talk?
Answer: I will talk about the culture, the sports, the restaurants and the scenery.
Questions to produce the next level:
  Culture: what were the key aspects of the culture?
  Sports: what are the main sports played in South Africa?
  Restaurants: what did I like about the restaurants?
  Scenery: what were the most notable beauty spots?

Note: In both the examples, we have only two levels. However there can be a third or a fourth, depending on the degree of detail you want to reach.

two examples of this

With the leadership model, we have at the second level 'listen' as one of the actions to take to support the follower. Posing the question, 'How do I learn to listen?' produces another level.

If the answer to 'What did I like about the restaurants?' was the excellent service, the variety of the food and the quality of the wines, the third-level questions might be:

  ▓ *The excellent service:* what were the specific features of this excellent service?
  ▓ *The variety of the food:* what examples can you provide?
  ▓ *The quality of the wines:* which were your favourites?

Two points need to be made before we move on. First, action-oriented headers are more powerful than topic headers; and second, you need to follow what is termed the MECE rule. ME stands for mutually exclusive. What this means is that at each level, no answer should be duplicated. If we look at the second-level answers, there is no duplication. If there is, it distracts readers and draws them away from your compelling case. CE stands for collectively exhaustive. This means that you should provide all the answers to each question, whatever the level. So at the keyline for leadership, if there were a glaring omission such as 'develop the follower', it would niggle away at the back of readers' minds, and, again, distract them from your case.

With structured thinking you can go from the top down, or start at the bottom with a list of items, or conclusion of research findings, and work back up. As an example, we look at the list of factors likely to characterise Head Office environments in the 1990s (the work on which this is based was carried out in the early 1990s – you can see how much is now true or changed!)

1.   Larger size of business.
2.   More senior managers and specialists at head office.
3.   One workstation for every staff member.
4.   Strong central computer department.
5.   Individual applications developed by users on workstations.
6.   Managers will do most of their own typing.
7.   Secretaries use workstations for more than word processing.
8.   Good information available to managers.
9.   Electronic messaging facilities.
10. Paper still used extensively.
11. A few important strategic applications in use.
12. Lower ratio of secretaries to professional staff.
13. IBM mainframes still in use.
14. Local communications network in head office.

The first step in going from the bottom up is to try to find groupings of the items that are connected by a common theme, then produce a summarising statement for each grouping. I provide an example on the next page:

the enlarged business will require a different organisation

■ Larger size of business (1).

■ More senior managers and specialists at head office (2).

■ Lower ratio of secretaries to professional staff (12).

■ Strong central computer department (4).

the IT facilities will change

■ One workstation for every member of staff (3).

■ Local communications network in head office (14).

■ IBM mainframes will still be used for a few strategic applications (11/13 neatly combined).

the new IT facilities will change the way people work

■ Secretaries will use workstations for more than word processing (7).

■ Managers will do most of their own typing (6).

■ Managers will have easy access to up-to-date information (8).

■ Electronic messaging facilities will be widely used, but will not replace paper (9/10 neatly combined).

■ Business staff will develop their own workstation-based applications (5).

Now you are in a position to think of the actual questions you have answered at the first and second level, and create the situation, complication and so on. Here is the final picture:

Situation: Examination of the head office environment in 1990s
Complication: Uncertainty as to impact of changes.
Key question: How will change impact on the environment?
Answer (governing thought): The head office environment will be different.

Level 1 generic question: In what ways?
Level 2 questions:
   What are the differences? (1, 2, 12, 4)
   How will the facilities change? (3, 14 and 11/13 combined)
   In what ways? (6, 7, 8, 9 and 10 combined, 5)

improving your performance

Here are two fascinating pieces of research to start with.

First, research was carried out using Yale University graduates in the United States. They were surveyed in the 1950s and again 20 years later. The research showed that 3 per cent were worth more in terms of wealth than the other 97 per cent put together. This 3 per cent also had better health and enjoyed better relationships with others.

Only one thing fully explained this 3 : 97 split. It was not parental wealth, degree subjects taken, career selected, ethnic origin, gender, or any other of the more obvious factors. The difference was that the 3 per cent had written goals in the 1950s while the huge majority had not.

Second, another research project was done in the 1970s by Richard Bandler and John Grinder (the creators of NLP – neuro-linguistic programming – from whence auditory, visual and kinaesthetic, to which we have already referred). They found that successful therapists were able to get their patients to define precisely what it would be like to be well. This definition is called a well-formed outcome.

Other research found that people who have achieved success in many different walks of life had well-formed outcomes or precisely written goals. Having such goals does not guarantee a successful outcome, of course. However it does lead to significantly better results by clear goal setters than similar people with vague goals. So we turn now to a methodology through which you can create well-formed outcomes and precisely written goals. We focus on improving your performance. To do this, we need to ask ourselves the right questions in the right sequence.

step 1 where do I want to focus and why?

We will only do something differently or better if we are committed to making the change – recognising and believing in the personal benefits we will gain, to compensate for the discipline and effort required.

We need to develop a series of goals or intentions framed in a positive action-oriented way, such as:

■ I will listen effectively.
■ I will project myself positively.
■ I will build an effective team.

I suggest you look back and select those leadership actions where you would like to get better. These can be things you already do well, rather than areas where you believe you do badly. Professor Drucker once said that it was a Western cultural defect to focus on weaknesses rather than to play to strengths.

step 2 how will I translate my intentions into objectives?

Objectives are concrete measures of progress towards achieving our goals/intentions. They need to be SMART (specific, measurable, agreed, realistic, time-related). A useful question to translate an intention into objectives is; 'What key change(s) or 'events' will indicate that the statement of intention is being achieved?'

Taking listening as an example: 'At the end of three months, when I ask for feedback from three colleagues (selected randomly!), each will confirm a significant improvement in my ability to listen to them.'

step 3   what should I do and when?

The final step is to develop an action plan. This means determining the sequence of actions to be taken and the deadlines that need to be met to achieve the objective(s). Additional questions to ask oneself at this stage can be:

- ■ Who can provide me with support and help?
- ■ How would I like that support to be given?
- ■ Who will be my 'external conscience' – to whom do I give explicit 'nagging rights?'

A final point is that persistence is the key to effective change. Research into behavioural change suggests that we need to practise new behaviours at least 13 times before they become a new habit: otherwise, we will revert to the established habit.

understanding your leadership orientation and style

Part of developing awareness is recognising where you currently are as a leader. However, it is insufficient simply to judge ourselves, as we may not see ourselves as others see us. We need to have feedback from those who observe us in our leadership role.

So first of all we look at perception gaps – how they arise and how they can be overcome – before asking you to complete a leadership questionnaire, and ask a work colleague to complete the same questionnaire, enabling you to determine his or her perception of your leadership orientation. From the results, you will be able to determine where your strengths lie, the direction of any gaps in perception, and how to close them, if they exist. An additional value from the questionnaire is the determination of your preferred leadership style. This chapter concludes by considering the link between leadership style and the delegation process.

perception gaps

In this section we provide a true story – a case study – of the extent of perception gaps that can arise between a leader and a follower. We consider how these gaps arise, and in the process, determine strategies for their elimination.

case study

In fact this is two true stories rolled into one, as the conversation with the bosses and one direct report of each boss were almost identical. In one instance, the boss was the group finance director of a multinational travel services company (and the direct report was a finance director), and in the other the boss was a main board director and chief executive officer of a manufacturing subsidiary, and the direct report was his marketing director.

Looking first at the conversation with the boss, with Q standing for questioner and B for boss, we have:

Q: So how would you describe your leadership style?
B: I think I would say I was an empowering leader who trusted his staff.
Q: An empowering, trusting leader – very powerful. How do you demonstrate this leadership approach?
B: It's simple, really. Let us say, a project crosses my desk, which I have neither the time nor the inclination to handle personally. I will call the appropriate person in, or to be honest, most of the time whoever is available, as we are all so busy these days, and say, 'I trust you and I empower you. Here's this little project for you to do. I know you will do an excellent job – best of luck', or some such thing. And what is more, usually a few days later I have some spare time on my hands, so I pop along to help him with the project.

Now to the follower's perspective:

Q: So how you would describe the kind of leadership you receive?

A: My boss is a dictator. (The other follower used the word 'tyrant'.)

Q: Oh dear! How does he demonstrate this dictatorial approach?

A: You know how overworked I am, with my increased responsibilities and number of direct reports. In the midst of trying to cope, I get the dreaded summons to the boss's office. Then I hear the two words I hate most in the English language, 'empower' and 'trust'. He waffles on about how he trusts me and is going to empower me, then dumps on me some Godawful project, which I haven't time to do, and sometimes haven't got the technical skill to do. Then he dismisses me with words like, 'I know you'll do a good job.' What do I do? I either dump it on – sorry, empower – one of my staff, or more often than not, as my staff are working all hours like me, I try my best to do the job. What is even worse is that a few days later, he saunters into my office, asks how I am getting on, reviews what I have done, and points out all my mistakes!

The existence of these perception gaps severely diminished the quality of the business relationships between the two bosses and their subordinates, as well as the competence and stress levels of all. Both bosses had to spend more time checking (or as was phrased, 'supporting') than was necessary, and the absence of coaching (for relevant projects) meant that mistakes were made and deadlines missed, which did not reflect well on the bosses in their superiors' eyes.

The followers had to work less effectively and efficiently than they would have done with proper coaching and support, which added to their stress levels. Additionally, they were seen as not sufficiently competent in the eyes of their bosses (despite the words uttered), which could affect their promotion prospects, or in these days of downsizing and/or organisational restructuring, prospects for continued employment.

how perception gaps arise

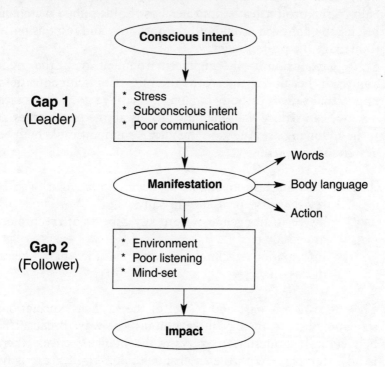

Figure 4.1 *How perception gaps arise*

You will notice that there are two gaps: the gap between conscious intention and manifestation (gap 1), and the gap between manifestation and the impact on the follower (gap 2). We are here looking specifically at the relationship between leader and follower, but the gaps and their causes hold for any relationship, business or social.

As an example, we shall take a situation where a boss wants to persuade a follower to change the way she is managing a project. Her conscious motivation or intent is to transfer a little of her expertise to Sally, say, so that she does the project better. As she is the boss and accountable for the results of the project, there is an element of self-interest. We will also assume that Sally is the project leader and her boss holds only a watching brief. Sally has been given both the authority and responsibility to manage the project team.

No gaps arise in the right environment with the right approach. Let us say the words the boss uses, with consistent non-verbal signals or body language, are, 'I've got a good idea how we can reduce the time taken to install the new network.' If the following are true, and the idea is sound, it is likely to be gratefully accepted:

- ▦ This suggestion comes as part of a regular weekly review of the project with Sally.
- ▦ There is an agenda, where key aspects of the project are discussed.
- ▦ Information technology (IT) is the item being discussed.

The suggestion is part and parcel of the explicit expectations set, and phrased in a positive non-critical way. Because the behavioural manifestation expresses the intent effectively, there is no gap type 1. With the environment also right, there is no gap type 2. The boss achieves her objective, which is to get Sally to 'change' – do something differently from what she would have done without this effective intervention. The suggestion is accepted because there is an environment where there is a 'shared voyage of discovery'. Sally will be coming through with her ideas as well, and both parties will be developing ideas together.

In the wrong environment, though there is no gap 1, we may cause a gap 2. We will return to this when we look at gap 2. We now focus on the causes of gap 1 and then how to eradicate them.

how the gap between intention and behavioural manifestation arises

We shall be looking at each possible cause in turn.

we are under stress

We may be under stress, feeling irritable, in a rush and so on. So we say, 'The installation time for the new network can be reduced by 50 per cent. This is what you have to do ...' Interestingly, when we are under stress or in a rush, and feeling the pressure, there is a natural inclination to move into a more 'tell' or 'command and control' leadership approach. However, some staff will only verbally agree and ignore the instruction afterwards. Others will do their level best to implement the suggestions or 'instructions', but they may not fully understand or 'own' the solution, so they implement them imperfectly.

In fact, Sally's manager might as well not bother with a face-to-face meeting, and send her an e-mail, advising her what to do to improve the management of her project. Putting yourself in Sally's shoes, would you see that intervention as a helpful suggestion, which acknowledges and respects her authority and competence as project leader? Yet that was the intent!

Incidentally there are many executives who use e-mails as a matter of course, with no intention to upset or demotivate, and no knowledge that that is the impact, because the follower is not prepared to volunteer feedback, which is never requested. One major factor in delegating or suggesting by e-mails is that we are clear in are own minds as to what we want and do not recognise that the person receiving the written message may not be clear. This is simply because the written word only contributes 7 per cent to effective communication. When we write we make assumptions without knowing it, and the other party cannot test them out.

example

One of the exercises managers enjoy the most on the development programmes I run is called the 'egg exercise'. Each team is provided with three pieces of white A4 paper, a pair of scissors, three strips of adhesive tape, a balloon and a raw egg. The team is given a specific brief via e-mail, and the facilitator is 'called away to a meeting' and so not available for further comment or clarification. The brief is, 'Using the equipment provided, launch the egg from the designated first-floor window so that it lands on the concrete below without cracking.'

We have an enormous range of offerings and successes. Many groups use the equipment provided and come up with a whole range of ingenious solutions, with eggs cradled in baskets or a cushion, or protected by a tripod underneath the balloon, or delicately placed at the top with cushioning devices such as cones or cylinders underneath.

Other groups do not use all the equipment, but probe the boundaries of the word 'launch'. One very elegant solution is to attach the egg to a very long strip of white paper, gently lower it to within a millimetre of the ground, then complete a successful 'launch'. Another is to have a member of the team go outside, catch the egg and place it gently on the ground. Some groups 'think outside the box' and use additional equipment to empty the egg of its contents, boil the egg, or fill the balloon with water and place the egg inside.

Finally one group, operating in a five-star hotel in Kuala Lumpur, ignored all the equipment, raided their bedrooms and rolled the egg down a number of sheets to the ground – successfully.

In the debriefing there are four main conclusions reached.

■ There is no one right answer, but a vast range of solutions to the given problem.
■ Where some groups have moved from the strict use of the equipment there is a perception of 'cheating' by those who did not, while the groups who did perceive themselves as having 'thought outside the box'.
■ It is recognised how much ambiguity there was in a two-line brief.
■ As the 'boss' I expected the one right answer I had in my mind, which I had not shared. The teams' proactivity and creativity to find a workable and effective solution had not helped our relationship!

we are driven by the subconscious

This is the second cause of the perception gap. A positive conscious intention may hide a subconscious or implicit intention that is more negative. So our conscious desire may be to improve the position, but to build self-esteem, we also want to criticise. The way we behave manifests such hidden intentions. 'Sally, your plan to install the new network is flawed. I have come up with a way to reduce installation time by 50 per cent. This is what you have to do.' Human nature being what it is, Sally is likely to pick the word 'flaw' as the key word in the sentences, and react negatively to what she perceives is implied criticism.

Incidentally, this cause is very common. I don't know if you have noticed, but often when two work colleagues get together to have a chat, or for that matter any two people in any setting, there can be a tendency to flatter each other and make the occasional unfavourable comment about anyone else not present whose name crops up. This combines positive and negative approaches to building self-esteem – building each other up and running others down to create a positive gap between ourselves and the other parties not present.

If we have low self-esteem as leaders, this negative manifestation of intent will be commonplace, though unrecognised, which is one reason it is so important to grow ourselves, particularly our self-esteem and confidence, as a precursor to effective leadership.

we communicate badly

The third cause is simply poor communication. An expert who knows more than Sally on IT matters (perhaps one of her team is the IT expert) might use language, jargon or concepts Sally does not fully understand. She might perceive the person as blinding her with science, or proving his or her superiority in the chosen area, even though these perceptions were not intended. Unless she acknowledges her lack of understanding and seeks and receives clarification (and often people are reluctant to expose ignorance), then implementation of the change will be not fully effective, or the wrong change will be implemented – neither of which are desirable outcomes.

In summary, if there is a gap 1, the manifestation of intent will produce an impact necessarily different from the intent. The other person accurately responds to the behaviour manifested, as that is the explicit demonstration of intent. She will assume, because of the gap, an intent that is consistent with the manifestation, but not the initiator's actual intent. Hence the misperception, which can be so damaging to relationships and to the effective initiation of change. In the example there is no gap 2.

how to close the gap

Looking at each cause in turn, we need to:

▦ Recognise and try to eliminate stress, at least temporarily. Avoid the hasty memo, sudden intervention by telephone, or 'dropping in'. In fact, as already suggested, what will help both our and our followers' stress levels significantly is to have a policy of proactively managing the environment so that it is conducive to the acceptance of our suggestion before we make our intentions known. However we may not be in a position to hold regular meetings, as our followers are geographically dispersed or the dictates of deadlines mean that we cannot wait. In such cases, it is better to telephone than to send an electronic message. This gives the chance for followers to question and clarify, and adds a further 38 per cent to the effectiveness of our communication.

▦ Deliberately use the 'assertive pause' to enable us to consciously consider our intention and motivations, and try to identify and eliminate any critical aspects before we speak.

▦ Try to avoid jargon, and, as a matter of policy, check that the other party has understood what she or he has agreed to.

how the gap between manifestation and impact arises

While manifestation of intent can be totally consistent with the intent, the environment in which the interchange occurs, the poor listening skills of the receiver, or his or her mind-set towards the transmitter, may mean that the actual impact is different from the intent or manifestation. We will look at each of these options in turn.

the leader enters the wrong environment

As already mentioned, the environment in which an inter-change takes place is critical to the outcome. So if the message is delivered in a way that is consistent in intention and manifestation, the impact can still be negative because the environment is wrong. Both the leader and the follower have a responsibility to manage the environment proactively. As suggested, the leader should avoid the unexpected, such as dropping by or telephoning with a new idea. Followers also need to be assertive when the leader enters the wrong environment, and advise him or her that they are rushed off their feet, busy in a meeting, about to go to a meeting, and so on.

the follower does not listen

The follower does not pick up the message correctly. There can be cause and effect with the environment. For example, the listener might be distracted by pressure of other work, or have failed to listen actively, and only focuses on part of the message, or picks up the wrong end of the stick.

This is no problem for leaders provided they do not make assumptions that agreement means understanding, and ensure those assumptions are checked. We can see that though, in theory, leaders can be considered as not responsible for the causes of gap 2, they need to be proactive to avoid the harmful effects. It is the price paid for being the leader.

the follower has a fixed mind-set

People will often not believe the evidence of their own eyes. It happens in personal relationships and in business relationships. People come to expect what happened in the past, and pass judgements, which become unwritten rules of behaviour towards the other person in the relationship. They do not notice changes in attitude or approach. So if followers perceive the initiator of change, their leader, as someone who has in the past criticised when suggesting change, told them what to do in a way that suffers from stress, or communicated poorly (in other words, there has always been a gap 1), they may well react to effective communication of intent as if there was still a gap!

This is a very difficult situation for the leader. Sally's boss, for instance, is likely to think, 'Here am I trying to respect Sally's position as project leader, suggesting a useful change in a positive way, and all she does is throw it back in my face. I am not standing for that. "Sally, let me tell you…"'

You may discover a direct way of handling this situation. All I can suggest is an avoidance strategy, the generic solution we considered at the beginning. If you, as leader, ensure that the environment is right, that itself will begin to change the perceptions of the person with the negative mind-set.

the cumulator

Finally we need to consider the cumulator: the combination of one or more causes of both gaps 1 and 2. They can combine in an explosive way, to lead to the most unfavourable outcomes, from a shouting match to employee dismissal. For instance, a leader's conscious intention might be to make a helpful intervention, but instead he or she criticises, and the intervention occurs in the wrong environment – in front of the follower's own subordinates. This is not deliberate by the initiator, who has rushed in to share a brainwave. The combination of gaps can produce explosive and damaging outcomes.

Such problems will be eliminated by adopting the generic solution – regular planned review meetings. It is also necessary to discipline oneself to recognise that in all but the most exceptional cases, there is no need to 'act in haste, and repent at leisure'.

It is vital that such perception gaps are reduced, if not eliminated, since they act as a considerable demotivator, as the example showed.

discover your leadership orientation

Tables 4.1 and 4.2 are two simple inventories, each consisting of 36 statements. Table 4.1 is for you to complete. Decide whether you agree or disagree with each statement, and put a cross in either the A or the D box. A decision must be made for each statement. Table 4.2 lists the identical statements, but this time it should be completed by a work colleague whose views you trust. Do not ask one of your followers to do this, since for cultural reasons followers may not be totally honest. Explain to the person you ask that he or she should give his/her view of how you operate in a leadership role at work.

Table 4.1 *Leadership orientation: own perception*

	A	D
1. I regularly check that my staff do what they say they will do		
2. I care about colleagues' feelings		
3. I believe team working is the best way to benefit from different individual approaches		
4. I find time to listen to colleagues' concerns and problems		

5. I ensure that targets, objectives and performance standards are agreed by the team as a whole

6. I discipline a member of staff who makes mistakes

7. I ensure that most decisions are taken by the team as a whole and not myself

8. I keep my staff under control

9. I am quick to praise another for their good performance

10. I am quick to criticise others when they make mistakes

11. I am trusting and trusted

12. I prefer to be part of group creativity sessions, rather than think creatively alone

13. I provide emotional support to colleagues

14. I am a co-ordinator rather than controller of my team

15. I find that if my staff are told exactly what is required and why, they will agree to do it

16. I prefer to work in a team rather than on my own

17. I use my authority to ensure that staff meet their targets

18. I have well-developed listening skills and am a good listener ☐ ☐

19. I encourage individuals in the group to share their feelings and expectations ☐ ☐

20. I develop a caring and supportive environment ☐ ☐

21. I believe that, when necessary, the judicious use of threats will get agreement ☐ ☐

22. I promote colleagues' ideas and suggestions as well as my own ☐ ☐

23. I persuade individuals in the group to share information and support each other ☐ ☐

24. I persuade others with the use of my authority and appropriate rewards and punishments ☐ ☐

25. I provide regular feedback to my staff on their performance ☐ ☐

26. I like to be in charge ☐ ☐

27. I help others create a shared vision and understanding ☐ ☐

28. I prefer working with a team to working with an individual ☐ ☐

29. I recognise the need to be sensitive to colleagues' feelings ☐ ☐

30. I discipline poor performers ☐ ☐

	A	D
31. I believe that the best agreement is when both sides win		
32. I push my views strongly		
33. I usually carry out communication and feedback in a team context		
34. I make my staff aware that I mean what I say, so they do what I request		
35. I openly express my thoughts and feelings, and encourage my staff to express theirs		
36. I am a catalyst and facilitator rather than a commander of my group		

Table 4.2 *Leadership orientation: another's perception*

He or she:	A	D
1. regularly checks that members of his or her staff do what they say they will do		
2. cares about colleagues' feelings		
3. believes team working is the best way to benefit from different individual approaches		
4. finds time to listen to colleagues' concerns and problems		
5. ensures that targets, objectives and performance standards are agreed by the team as a whole		

6. disciplines a member of staff who makes mistakes ☐ ☐

7. ensures that most decisions are taken by the team as a whole ☐ ☐

8. keeps the staff under control ☐ ☐

9. is quick to praise others for their good performance ☐ ☐

10. is quick to criticise others when they make mistakes ☐ ☐

11. is trusting and trusted ☐ ☐

12. prefers to be part of group creativity sessions rather than think creatively alone ☐ ☐

13. provides emotional support to colleagues ☐ ☐

14. is a co-ordinator rather than controller of the team ☐ ☐

15. finds that if staff are told exactly what is required and why, they will agree to do it ☐ ☐

16. prefers to work in a team rather than on his/her own ☐ ☐

17. uses his/her authority to ensure that staff meet their targets ☐ ☐

18. has well-developed listening skills and is a good listener ☐ ☐

19. encourages individuals in the group
    to share their feelings and expectations ☐ ☐

20. develops a caring and supportive
    environment ☐ ☐

21. believes that, when necessary, the
    judicious use of threats will get
    agreement ☐ ☐

22. promotes not just his/her own ideas and
    suggestions but also those of colleagues ☐ ☐

23. persuades individuals in the group to
    share information and support each other ☐ ☐

24. persuades others with the use of their
    authority and appropriate rewards
    and punishments ☐ ☐

25. provides regular feedback to their staff on
    their performance ☐ ☐

26. likes to be in charge ☐ ☐

27. helps others create a shared vision and
    understanding ☐ ☐

28. prefers working with a team to working
    with an individual ☐ ☐

29. recognises the need to be sensitive
    to colleagues' feelings ☐ ☐

30. disciplines poor performers ☐ ☐

31. believes that the best agreement is
    when both sides win ☐ ☐

32. pushes his/her own views strongly

33. usually carries out communication and feedback in a team context

34. makes staff aware that what is said is meant, and that they should do what is requested

35. openly expresses his/her own thoughts and feelings, and encourages members of staff to express theirs

36. is a catalyst and facilitator rather than a commander of the group

Once you have both inventories completed, you can proceed to scoring. Table 4.3 is the scoring chart. Take the inventory you completed, look at the three 'self' columns ('controlling', 'supporting' and 'team'), and circle the numbers of the statements for which you put an 'Agree' (and only an 'Agree'). Total the circles at the bottom of each of the three columns. In the example in Table 4.4, the totals are 4, 10 and 8 (out of a maximum of 12). You can graph your numbers on the empty chart provided. The manager in the sample has a self-perception as low on 'controlling', very high on 'supporting', and high on 'team'.

Then repeat the scoring for your colleague's answers, using the 'other' columns, to get a complete picture, including the extent and location of any differences of perception. The sample manager's 'other' profile is (8, 6, 4), so the colleague sees this person as strong in 'control', moderate in 'support' and low in 'team'. The differences are {−4, 4 ,4}. In this case there are significant gaps between the individual's self-perception as a leader and the colleague's perception.

Table 4.3 *Leadership orientation: scoring the inventories*

Controlling		Supporting		Team	
Self	Other	Self	Other	Self	Other
1	1	2	2	3	3
6	6	4	4	5	5
8	8	9	9	7	7
10	10	11	11	12	12
15	15	13	13	14	14
17	17	18	18	16	16
21	21	20	20	19	19
24	24	22	22	23	23
26	26	25	25	27	27
30	30	29	29	28	28
32	32	31	31	33	33
34	34	35	35	36	36

Total

Difference

Before we use the data to consider leadership style, let me set out the broad interpretation of different profiles, looking briefly at profiles where there is agreement (no or a one point difference) and then at those where there are perception gaps.

where there is correlation

To deal with team orientation first, the higher the score, the greater the individual's ability to build an effective team. If your score is very low (say 3 or less), and especially if you are high in control and low in support, I would recommend you find some way to experience effective team work (perhaps a short external programme, open to other managers from other

Table 4.4

	Controlling		Supporting		Team	
	Self	Other	Self	Other	Self	Other

Self (4, 10, 8)   Other (8, 6, 4)   Difference (−4, 4, 4)

An example of a completed scoring chart for the leadership orientation inventories

	Controlling		Supporting		Team	
	Self	Other	Self	Other	Self	Other

Self (, ,)   Other (, ,)   Difference (, ,)

A blank scoring sheet

organisations, and with none of your colleagues in attendance). This will provide you with both belief in teams and the ability to build an effective team. (Additionally Chapter 7 may help you.)

If you have moderate to low control, moderate to high support, and moderate to high team orientation, you have all that is required to build an effective team.

If you have very low control, and very high support and team orientation, you may have problems with decision taking. During team building you need to control the process (this is covered in more detail in Chapter 7). Afterwards you need to make decisive interventions when a change disrupts the team dynamics.

Excluding the team dimension, if the scores in support are very low (3 or less) or control very high (9 or more), the implication is that you are too oriented to 'command and control'. If both scores are very high, while you have allowed your followers a certain amount of development, you have never learnt when to let go. You need to develop flexibility of style with individual followers, and adapt your style according to given situations. This is covered in the next section.

where there are perception gaps

Which is more relevant to leadership effectiveness, how we see ourselves, or how others see us? I think the latter. Of course, the direction of the gap is important. If you see yourself as moderate in team orientation and are seen by your colleague as high in this dimension, you are simply more effective a team manager than you thought yourself to be. It is important to accept the good news, because we get even better only if we explicitly recognise and develop strength.

Conversely if, as happens, you see yourself as very strongly team-oriented but are not perceived as such by your colleague, you need to look within the two sets of answers to identify the specific areas of disagreement. If you trust the colleague who completed the inventory sufficiently, it is worth exploring the specifics with him or her. This will tell you in more detail what specific areas you need to be aware of, and what weaknesses you should try to counter.

The same holds for gaps in the other two orientations. A very weak perceived rating for 'support' is a cause of concern. The extremes of strongly perceived control, and low ratings for support and team orientation, suggest a leader who is permanently focused on managing tasks, not leading people; and/or someone who is focusing on him or herself and not those being led, because of a lack of confidence and self-belief, which is often a subconscious reality.

discover your leadership style

Models of four leadership styles have been developed by a number of experts. I will use the one developed by Kenneth Blanchard, writer of *The One Minute Manager*. First you need to find out which of the four styles or style combinations you currently prefer, and compare your verdict with your colleague's perception. We then explain each style, when it is appropriate to use which, and look at how effective delegation can be seen as a progression of styles.

completing the chart

Figure 4.2 shows the completed chart, using the sample scores shown earlier, of {4,10} for 'own perception' (we ignore the team score for this analysis) and {8,6} for 'other perception'. This manager sees him/herself as S3, and is seen by the completer of the other form as a combination of S2/S1. Please use Figure 4.3 to enter your own scores.

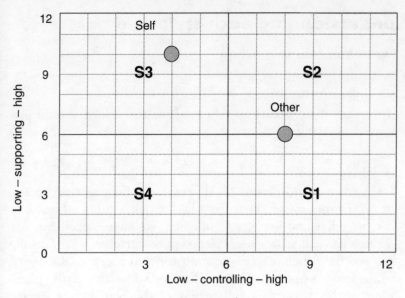

Figure 4.2 *Leadership style example*

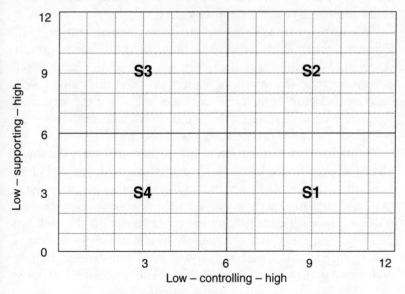

Figure 4.3 *Leadership style: yours*

understanding each style

We look at each style in turn.

S1: tell

There are three occasions when we, as the leader, should use the S1 'tell' style:

a crisis

If there is a crisis, it is our role to resolve it. Imagine the captain of the Titanic, when the iceberg had struck, calling all his officers together and saying, 'Gentlemen, we have a problem. An iceberg has just struck us. So let us pour ourselves a stiff drink, eh, and have a chin-wag – a brainstorm to promote discovery of the various options. Then we'll spend some time action planning, with of course a full review of the plan before implementing it. It's 3 pm, and if we get started now, we should be ready for effective action in four hours!'

Of course not. As leaders, we seize control and tell our followers what to do, why and how, so the crisis is rapidly resolved. I would emphasise that we should not simply tell people what to do, as some leaders do. We must also give a clear explanation of the crisis or reason requiring the action we suggest. Nor is covering 'what' and 'why' sufficient: we must give clear guidance on the specifics of the 'how'.

'Gentlemen, we have been hit by an iceberg. We must abandon ship immediately with a minimum of panic. Harry, you will be responsible for managing the news to the passengers and organising their move to the lifeboats; George, you will be responsible for getting the passengers into the lifeboats and lowering them to the sea, applying the principle of women and children first; Charles, you will send out distress signals: Matthew, you will ...' (and so on). 'The sequence I propose is.... Any questions, ladies and gentlemen? No? Then proceed to action.'

a follower new to a role

Where a specific follower is new to a job, and likely to lack confidence and be feeling insecure, then we need to 'tell' in a constructive way – provide clear guidance on what needs to be done, why and how, and monitor performance. We should also provide a measure of support by having an open door policy if the person runs into difficulties, to encourage the follower to develop. It is an excellent idea to suggest he or she has thought through any problems encountered before coming to see you. This enables an adult/adult conversation about solutions to take place and not the continuation of the parent/child relationship.

sudden negative change

We will look at this in more detail in Chapter 8 on change. However sudden change, perceived negatively, can cause a loss of self-esteem, uncertainty and negative emotions. The leader needs to take control of the situation to avoid the team splitting at the seams, or the individual becoming demotivated and incompetent.

S2: coaching

This style is used where a follower has gained a degree of competence and confidence. While we provide the what and why, we will involve the follower in the how, seek his or her input, and listen to the views expressed, so there is a genuine dialogue on and agreement to the implementation. We should also make ourselves available if the person runs into difficulties.

S3: supporting

This is used when we have confident and competent followers who can do the job well. So we advise them what they need to do and why, but trust them to determine for themselves the how. We remain in touch, by having an open door policy and being available to support if problems or unexpected difficulties are encountered.

S4: delegating

This is a style especially used at higher levels in an organisation, when the leader expects lieutenants to be able to run the part of the organisation for which they are responsible, and provides little direction or support. Without the use of the earlier styles, as appropriate, this style is known as 'dumping'.

five key points to conclude:

- The progression through the four leadership styles can be viewed as a process to effective delegation or empowerment, and we should attempt this development path for all our followers, as then we are optimising our own time usage. We save more time if we remain locked into an S1 or S1/S2 combination, and we will be able to concentrate much more on the strategic aspects of our job.
- If you refer back to the 20 actions suggested for effective leaders, then the list under 'develop the follower' can be seen as a progression through from S1 to S4.
- There is a need to avoid developing mindsets or acting on false assumptions.

case study

I talked to a partner in a City law firm about one of his senior associates, who was coming on a development programme. The partner was extremely enthusiastic. 'He is a star. He is on the fast track to partnership and he deserves it. He is no trouble at all. Any work I give to him, he does to a very high standard and always by the deadline, which can be very tough, as some of our clients are very demanding indeed. I don't have to spend any time with him and never have to go through his drafts with him to point out all his mistakes. This is not the case with all my other associates, which is why he is a star, as he knows and all his colleagues know.'

I then talked to the senior associate, and discovered one of the unhappiest people I had ever met. To paraphrase his words, 'I am at my wit's end. I get no support or praise from my partner – I hardly ever see him. He just dumps work on me and lets me get on with it. I am very isolated, as all my peers know I am on the fast track to partnership, so I have lost the few friends I had. What is even worse is that I get given assignments to complete that require a technical skill level I lack. I have no one to turn to for help. My partner is always going on about his other associates asking him stupid questions, and I simply cannot admit ignorance to him. I wouldn't be his bloody little star if I did. I can't consult any of my colleagues, as they resent me because I am going to make partner ahead of them, so I can't ask and they wouldn't answer. What do I do? I start going mad. I am already around 2,400 chargeable hours, with my target at 1,600, as I get lumbered with all the high-profile deals my partner cannot handle. On top of that I have to spend hours and hours at night (when I am not doing an all-nighter on a deal) looking up all the precedents and studying all the know-how documents to get the answers to the technical areas I don't understand. I have no friends, no partner, no sex life, no time for myself – nothing except work, work, work and more work.'

The lesson for the leader is to always ask the follower whether there are any aspects of the job being delegated where he or she might need additional guidance or training to help him or her succeed.

- If we recognise the level of confidence and ability of our followers, and the nature of the situation they face, we can then choose the leadership style that is appropriate. By doing this we develop a flexible and appropriate response.
- Research into the collective views of leaders and their followers suggests that there is a significant gap in perception on leadership styles. Followers usually see us operating one level lower than we think we are ourselves. The vast majority of managers who have

completed the appropriate questionnaire, and have had the questionnaire completed by a follower or followers, see themselves as operating with an S2/S3 combination and are seen as operating as S1/S2. The two leaders in the case study that began this chapter saw themselves as S2/S3, and were seen as alternating between S4 (dumping) and a poor S1 (simply monitoring – 'pointing out all our mistakes').

developing core leadership skills

In this chapter we look at the two core skills of effective leaders – listening and questioning.

listening

Have you ever been in a situation (and I would be very surprised if you had not), when you were talking and the person you were talking to clearly was not listening to a word you said? Can you recall, looking back, how you felt about this?

When developing listening skills in managers, this is one of the first exercises. The managers are put into pairs. One is briefed to talk for two minutes on something he or she is passionate about, and the other to do everything in his or her power, bar walking from the room, to indicate lack of listening: for example avoiding eye contact, watching someone else, or fidgeting. When we debrief the exercise, we ask the same question we asked you. A typical set of answers are:

▓ I was angry and annoyed with the listener (one manager used the word 'hated' once).
▓ The listener showed complete lack of respect.
▓ I lost concentration.
▓ I felt a fool.
▓ I found that I was repeating what I had said previously.
▓ I felt confidence and self-esteem drain away.

Ineffective listening by a leader, especially if it becomes a habit, is the single greatest way to destroy the relationship with the follower. This is why, I guess, it was top of the list of desired attributes. It was also the one with the greatest gap! Conversely, listening effectively to a follower is the single greatest way to build the relationship. In the Bible it says, 'It is better to give, than to receive'. To develop good relationships with anyone, it is better to listen than to talk.

One reason is that, by listening, we are showing interest, and everyone warms to anyone who shows interest in him or her. More importantly, we are saying, without using a single word, 'I think you are an important human being, whose opinions and thoughts I value.' We give people respect, we build their confidence and self-esteem. They will reciprocate (especially to someone who is in a leadership position for them) and we will have started on the virtuous path to an effective business relationship.

So having established the vital importance of listening, we answer the three key questions:

▓ Why is listening difficult?
▓ How can we identify poor listening?
▓ How can we become effective listeners?

why is listening difficult?

There are six reasons:

talkers are rewarded

Most of us learnt as babies that making a noise brought attention. As children, the noisiest and loudest often became the leaders and innovators of childhood games and activities. In formal education, those children who always answered questions and spoke clearly and distinctly were more favoured and praised. In adult and business life, the pattern continues. Those who make the most noise often gain more attention than they or their opinions deserve. Talkers are rewarded.

we are more important

Sometimes we say to ourselves, though rarely at the conscious level, that we are more important than the follower to whom we are talking. This is understandable, as we all need to build our self-esteem and one way is to feel superior to the individual with whom we are conversing. This reality can be reinforced given our 'superior' status. If we think we are more important, whether consciously or not, we will not listen actively.

we are more knowledgeable

A little knowledge is a dangerous thing. A lot of knowledge can be even more dangerous, when it comes to listening. It is a variation of the perception of importance reason – but this time it is a perception not that the follower to whom we are talking is not important, but that what he or she has to say – the content – is not important. We know more than our follower, and say to ourselves, deep down: 'Those who know nothing, have nothing to say.' Innocence and ignorance can be the source of much creativity and subsequent knowledge. Many inventions have come into being because somebody did not know 'It can't be done' or did not accept 'This is the way we do things round here' and somebody else listened.

However, most of us succumb individually and collectively to the 'new boy syndrome'. 'Until you have earned your spurs, proved your competence, you have nothing to say.'

we think faster than the follower speaks

This means that we have time available, which can be put to good use by concentrating and trying to fully comprehend what is being said to us, or to bad use by allowing distractions and our own thoughts to intrude.

we develop our mind-sets

From the moment of our birth we enter an uncertain world, with a complexity and a dynamic we can never comprehend. We are therefore driven, whether consciously or not, to manage that uncertainty. Some of us are capable of tolerating, even enjoying, high levels of ambiguity and uncertainty, but for all of us there is a degree and intensity that is unbearable.

To enable us to cope, we create and confirm areas of certainty – beliefs, assumptions, attitudes and opinions that we do not consciously question. If we did, we would raise the level of uncertainty in our lives. We would be taking a risk, as we do not know what is the breaking point for us.

The stronger our mind-sets, which are likely to increase in this age of increasing uncertainty, the more we can only listen to ourselves. We need to carry out a conscious and deliberate act of control and commit to change, before we can ask the right question and listen effectively to the answers.

the talker communicates poorly

The fault does not always lie with the listener. We can be poor speakers. We can speak too quickly. We can send out too much information. We can send out veiled messages with unsuitable speech patterns, or mixed messages, using body language inconsistent with the words we speak. A follower who does this makes it difficult for us as listener.

This is a key skill of an effective questioner – to use the power of questions to ensure the messages received are clear to us, and in the process, clarify them for the follower. Questioning is considered in the next section.

how we can identify poor listening

If we can identify poor listening in ourselves, we can improve. If we identify poor listening in the follower, we can rectify the situation. We should not only listen effectively to the follower, but ensure the messages we transmit are picked up effectively.

At the heart of poor listening is body language – the non-verbal signals transmitted, the gestures we make or postures we take up. But language has also a part to play. There are six useful classifications.

aggressive listening

There are two types, deliberate and accidental. Deliberate aggressive listening occurs when we do not want to listen, but we have been forced to listen, because of, say, a direct emotional request. We have responded aggressively. Our heart is not in it, and we feel resentful. We fold our arms, presenting a barrier to the receipt of information, have a stiff posture and tend to glare.

The only way to avoid deliberate aggressive listening is not to be aggressive! On a more practical level, we can deploy the 'assertive pause'. If we receive a request we did not anticipate, we are automatically likely to respond emotionally. If we do not like the request, the emotions will be negative, and in this case of a direct request, we will fall into aggressive listening. The 'assertive pause' is simply pausing and not responding straightaway. While we pause, we should try to breathe out through the rib-cage, hold our breath and only breathe shallowly (though the rib-cage) for a moment. By using the assertive pause, we will think more clearly, control the immediate negative emotional reaction and respond with effective questions and active listening.

Accidental aggressive listening occurs when we feel we ought to be listening, we want to listen, but are not very skilled at 'active listening' and try too hard. We feel the need to verbally reassure the follower, 'Yes, I am listening to you!' which is a give-away to the follower that we are not! Our concentration at the conscious level makes us lean forward (perhaps invading the follower's body space unintentionally) with a stiff posture, and what we think is an interested look is perceived as a discomfiting stare. The only way to avoid this type of aggressive listening, because it is not conscious, is to practise active listening.

passive listening

This is a very common form of poor listening. It is when we have no desire to speak, have resigned ourselves to listen (perhaps the follower likes to hear the sound of his or her own voice), and we drift off slumped in the chair, body half-turned away from the speaker, hand over mouth to conceal the occasional yawn, and little eye contact as we tend to look elsewhere. If we catch ourselves out in this mode, we need to snap to attention, interrupt the listener and own up, along the lines of, 'Very sorry, I missed your last point. Could you run it by me again?'

listening interruptus

This is where we do not want to listen, we want to speak. In the early stages, assuming we cannot find an appropriate moment to interrupt, we are likely to fidget in some fashion, such as drumming our fingers or playing with a pencil (assuming that is not the way we display nerves). Then we lean forward, and interrupt.

Often, both parties can be in this mode simultaneously. The result is a bewildering dance of never-completed statements or themes, as the talking prize is snatched one from the other, and back again. The bodies move forward when talking and back as the threatened invasion of personal body space forces the involuntary move. The occasional fidget manifests itself if the unnatural state of silence is too prolonged.

The only way to avoid this is developing the right mind-set or attitude in advance of the conversation, and the questioning skill to close down the verbiage of the follower.

logical listening

This is where we listen with our minds, and not our hearts. We are deaf to the messages conveyed by the way the follower speaks the words, and the non-verbal signals provided. We hear and respond to the words only. 'I'm getting divorced' receives the reply, 'Then get a lawyer.'

Logical listening is often the precursor to passive listening. We start semi-detached because we are only operating at the logical and not the emotional level. We are quick with the obvious logical solutions, become bored and lapse into passive listening.

Logical listening can also be the precursor to aggressive listening. Followers want to share the feelings behind the verbal messages they make, and are quite capable of working out the logical responses for themselves. They pick up the lack of eye contact, and the lack of warm, supportive body language, which compound their sense of irritation provided by the statement of the obvious. Assuming the conversation has not been terminated, they will often make the emotional appeal, 'You are just not listening to me.' We will then have the direct, emotional response (perceived negatively) which can trigger aggressive listening, in the absence of that 'assertive pause'.

arrogant listening

When we feel very comfortable and confident, often in front of a follower, we can adopt this posture – hands clasped behind our heads, leaning back, legs stretched forward or even on a desk (at work) or stool (at home), as we gaze at the ceiling or down our noses. It does not necessarily display arrogance: when we are on our own, we could just be thinking. But it does if we are with a follower, and are supposed to be listening.

It is a posture that many of us adopt, but are resistant to recognising as having arrogant overtones. It is interesting to note how we automatically remove our feet from the desk, and change our stance, when our own boss comes in. In some oriental cultures, where the cult of the individual is less strong, it causes a personal affront if you display the soles of the feet to a business colleague or acquaintance.

It is a self-centred style of 'listening', based on an assumption of superiority, and is very passive, as there is complete disinterest at both the logical and emotional levels. The body language is static, as the posture will be maintained whether we talk or listen. There is no positive eye contact, although we do not mind 'looking down our noses', the only way we can look in that position.

If our attention is eventually caught, then we will alter our postures and gestures, depending on whether we move into logical listening, aggressive listening, or listening interruptus. If we take that deep breath, recognise what are we are doing and why, we can move into active listening.

nervous listening

We manifest this when we are in an awkward situation – a job interview, appraisal interview, talking to a 'difficult boss' or client and so on. Occasionally we might manifest this with a follower, if we are being put under pressure.

We want to listen, we try to listen, but are only capable of listening to our heartbeat. This form of non-listening manifests itself by nervous gestures, which are also displayed when we have to talk. There are an almost infinite number of nervous gestures, and each person has a favourite. We usually do not know we are making them. It is a matter of great surprise to managers when they see themselves on video for the first time to recognise this reality. We fiddle with our fingers, we fiddle with our hair, we fiddle with our faces, we cover our mouths and move the forefinger up and down our top lips, we tap-dance under the table, we move our chairs and tickle our ears. The list goes on and on.

As an aside, developing the ability to notice another's involuntary gestures and hence nervousness is a useful skill. If we want to generate empathy, we know we have a lot of work to do. If there has been verbal agreement to something we have said, we know that it was an involuntary agreement, unlikely to transfer into action.

Our nervous listening will also be conveyed by the fact that we ask for information to be repeated, because we have not heard it properly, or by coming in with the answer to the wrong question.

As nervous listeners, there is little we can do, except take that deep breath or breaths to calm ourselves. When the follower is behaving in this annoying manner, remember that it may well be nerves and try to calm him down.

A final point – often we try to control our nerves and our gestures, and partially succeed. Assuming we are sitting down, the gestures move to our feet (the tap-dance or shuffle), which cannot be seen. What a keen observer will notice is that we adopt a very rigid posture above the table.

how we can become better listeners

There are seven key ways to becoming better listeners.

be committed

We need to recognise and believe in the power of effective listening – that unless we listen effectively, we have wasted all those good questions. We have to want to listen 'actively'. 'Actively' is an excellent word, because it conveys the reality that we have to take a conscious act to listen well. As we now know, effective listening is not a passive thing, a meaning the word conveys, but a difficult skill, in which we need to engage our hearts and minds actively if we are going to be effective and reap the rewards of our questions.

be objective

We need to think, make that deliberate pause, and take that deep breath. As we have seen, it is our feelings, our opinions, our prejudices (whether against the follower or the content) or our nerves that deny us effective listening.

Just as good leaders learn how to take control, not of others, but of themselves, so too does the effective listener. Taking the time out as a discussion starts to say to ourselves, 'I am going to listen' will improve our skill. Deliberately pausing when a comment comes that triggers an instant negative logical or emotional response will improve our skill. In short, we need to be proactive, not reactive. Only when we have listened to ourselves can we listen effectively to the follower.

suspend judgement

If we judge, we don't really listen. If we judge in the act of listening, there are two outcomes. First, we disagree. If we don't want to express our disagreement, we will be turned off and lapse into passive listening, thus denying an effective conversation. This passive listening, if we are in the follower role, can lead to the outcome (which annoys so many bosses because they don't understand the reasons) where we verbally commit to doing things we don't believe in or want to do. As a result we either do them badly or not at all, if we can find a good excuse later.

If we do express our disagreement, we will move into aggressive listening or listening interruptus, and the subsequent flow from us of closed questions will deny an effective conversation.

Second, we agree. That may seem fine, but early agreement will lose some little nuances or new angles that are lost because we have stopped listening.

check for understanding

How often do both parties assume understanding, only to be rudely awakened subsequently by actions inconsistent with the understanding assumed? So pause to recap. Summarise the key points the talker has made and get agreement from the talker before moving on. Clarify and confirm your understanding.

use positive body language

The words we speak have only 7 per cent of the total impact in face-to-face communication. The way we speak – the tones, modulation, intensity, phrasing and use of pauses – has 38 per cent of the total impact, and our body language – our gestures, posture and facial expression – a highly significant 55 per cent.

If we are listening effectively, then we will display the right body language. If we consciously try to use the right body language, we will probably feel awkward, but we will be better listeners – 'conscious incompetence' will lead with practice to 'conscious competence' and eventually 'unconscious competence' or natural ability. Rubbish, I hear some of you say. Not at all. It is why people being trained in good telephone technique are told to smile. When they do, their tone of voice becomes warmer, and this is picked up at the other end of the phone.

So let us consider facial expression, gestures and body posture.

facial expression

The facial expressions should reflect the feelings being expressed. If the follower is feeling sad, look sad; if happy, look happy; and if angry, look angry – angry together at the source of the speaker's anger.

If you are the source of anger, that's a different kettle of fish. The speaker will get the impression that you are angry with her, which is likely to be the case. This is the moment for the assertive pause, not the angry response.

If there are no emotions being expressed, as the speaker is in logical mode, then look confident and thoughtful – you are both in thinking mode together.

There should be fairly frequent eye contact, but never a glare nor stare. Such eye contact stops you becoming distracted, and conveys the message that you are, in fact, all ears.

gestures
Gestures are for the speaker, and not the listener. If appropriate gestures are used, the impact of the speaker's message is significantly enhanced. Gestures from the listener act as a distraction – a form of non-verbal interruption.

posture
There is not a single right posture, as the posture will vary according to the situation – the logic or emotion being expressed, the ebb and flow of the conversation. However, in all situations, an assertive posture should be adopted, not an aggressive nor submissive one. For instance, when seated, the listener could take up an open position (neither legs nor arms folded), leaning forward slightly, with the head a little to one side, and hands clasped loosely together, resting on the lap.

There are variations, such as leaning back slightly (to accommodate the other person leaning forward), open posture, with one hand on the chin and the other supporting the elbow or sitting straight with legs slightly apart, each hand resting on the appropriate knee. This last position is the best position for the back, and is known as the Pharaoh's posture.

Another way of deciding an effective posture is to consciously avoid all the postures we have covered under poor listening.

use words
An effective listener uses words in the right tone to convey the right meaning. There are two aspects, reflection and interest. As we have seen, we should use our faces to reflect the speaker's feelings. Equally, our words and tone can support this

by paraphrasing the words or reflecting the feeling of the speaker. Show interest by those little verbal noises or even words. The murmur 'mmmmhuh' (or variations, which I will not try to spell) or 'Well, I never' or simply 'I agree.'

appreciate silence

We tend to dislike silence, and rush in verbally to fill it. In fact, silence can be a very powerful way to uncover truth. At a judicious moment, when we have asked a searching question and received a short, unsatisfactory response, or we have made a telling statement, we fall silent until the follower speaks. What will often happen is that followers will reveal what they have tried to conceal.

They rush in to fill that awkward pause. They are very consciously concerned at the silence. They are emotionally distracted, and what they were trying consciously to conceal slips out, or, at the very least, a veil is removed, which, if we are listening effectively, we can pick up and probe.

However, this reality has more to do with effective interviewing skills than with effective listening skills. The main point is that a natural discomfort with silence may often impair our active listening, either because we do not pause to collect our thoughts and give a measured response – ask the right question – or we speak when it would have been better from the other person's point of view if we had remained silent.

We can, by being silent, give the other person time to control emotions or gather thoughts, or simply share together a pleasant mood or ambience. As Mozart said, 'Silence is the most profound sound in music.'

Before we move on to look at questioning, there is one final aspect to listening, referred to as reflective listening, a very powerful way to deal with someone who is under the grip of emotion. When someone communicates with us, there are only three things they can communicate – feelings, facts and needs.

We will take, as an example, the situation when an internal or external client has phoned up and complained angrily that we have not met an agreed deadline and he or she needs the vital document right away. Most managers from most cultures in this situation do not acknowledge the emotion, but deal with the facts and needs, often justifying a 'mistake'. 'Sorry to have missed the deadline – our IT systems crashed yesterday and the document will be with you in a few hours.' Typically, the lack of any acknowledgement of the emotions that are driving the client means that he or she continues to complain and remains angry.

The emotion should be acknowledged first, and the phrasing should overstate rather than understate the emotion. The British particularly are prone to understatement, which adds fuel to the flames. 'I can see you are a little upset' leads to 'I am not a little upset, I am really angry!' However, 'I can see you are absolutely furious' puts the client on the back foot. 'Well, I am not furious – I am very annoyed.' We can continue, 'Yes, I can see that, and I understand your feelings.' Then pause. The client is calming down and losing the negative emotion, because it has been explicitly acknowledged and understood. Only when the client has moved from the emotional to the rational should you attempt to deal with his or her need. Then you can simply say, 'I apologise for missing the deadline. The document will be couriered to your offices and arrive within two hours.'

What often happens is that if the emotion is listened to first and then the need addressed, the client is happy. Clients are very busy, as we are, and will treat the episode as closed and move on to the next item on a crowded agenda. What we tend to do is to justify ourselves and answer questions that are not asked. So only provide the explanation for the missed deadline if the client, in this instance, asks for one.

Finally, remember that just as bad listening destroys the power of the right question, without the right question, you have little opportunity to listen actively. The two skills are inextricably interlinked. If you want to improve the quality of and effectiveness of all your key relationships (not only the relationship with your followers) you have to develop both questioning and listening skills in tandem.

questioning

We start by providing one example of ineffective questioning and one of effective questioning, then analyse the examples to discover the keys to effective questioning, enabling us to develop our followers and improve our relationships with them.

questioning ineffectively

We eavesdrop on a conversation between boss (B) and subordinate (S), which may have met the boss's objectives, but completely demotivated the employee.

B: Chris tells me that you were late again this morning. Is that correct?
S: Yes. I'm very sorry.
B: In fact, you were half an hour late. Am I right?
S: Yes. (mumbled)
B: To be completely accurate (and you know that I like to have my facts right), you have been half an hour late every day this week, have you not?
S: Yes.
B: This firm does not tolerate laziness and unpunctuality. I am a fair man (as you know), but I don't beat about the bush. If this occurs once more, we will start the disciplinary procedures against you. Do I make myself clear?
S: Yes.
B: Well, don't let it happen again.

questioning effectively

We re-run the conversation, but this time with a boss who has learnt what are the right questions and how to ask them.

B;   Chris tells me that you were half an hour late this morning, and, in fact, every morning this week. Is that correct?

S: Yes. I'm very sorry.

B: Tell me, why were you late?

S: The traffic's been very bad.

B: But the traffic's always bad, and you normally come to work on time. So what's the problem?

S: My mother's very poorly.

B: I'm sorry to hear that, John. It must be very tough for you, as you are very close to your mother.

S: Yes, Alex, it's tough all right.

B: (pause) But I don't see why you are late, John.

S: Well, mother now needs our full-time care. She can't be left on her own for a minute. Barbara, my wife, works nights and doesn't get back home until half-past eight. I set off immediately for work, but because of the traffic, I'm late.

B: I see. And when do you leave to go home?

S: I have to leave at the normal time to relieve Barbara, but I have cut my lunch time to half an hour, to make up the time that way.

B: I see. I've no problem with that at all.

analysing the conversations

In the first conversation, the boss asked four questions – all closed. Closed questions produce yes or no answers. Here we have – Is that? Am I? Have you? Do I? In the re-run, the boss used two closed question and four open questions. As Rudyard Kipling wrote:

I keep six honest serving men.
They taught me all I knew;
Their names are What and Why and When,
And How and Where and Who.

Of the six basic open questions, 'What?' 'Why?' and 'How?' promote discovery, and the use of them is the key to creativity, coaching and relationship development. 'Where?', 'When?' and 'Who?' establish facts. The primary uses of closed questions are to:

▧ Confirm facts.
▧ Acknowledge emotion.
▧ Push for a decision, such as 'Will you marry me?'
▧ Avoid a conversation. With our increasingly busy work lives, pressures on time and erosion of the work/life balance, we should consciously decide when we want to spend the time in a meaningful conversation and the reverse. How often do we say to a colleague at the beginning of the working week, 'How was your weekend?' and they tell us in all the gruesome detail. Far better to plan and implement the closed route: 'Did you have a good weekend?' If the answer is 'Yes', we are off the hook. If it is 'No', we have a let-out clause. 'Sorry to hear that – catch you later for the details – must dash for my meeting (or whatever) – bye.'

However we all, with very rare exception, have a tendency to ask far too many closed questions. I recall briefing a group of managers, who had all recognised the power of and how to use probing sequences of the 'discovery queens'. One of them was to share a real issue or concern, and another (they were in groups of three with one in the observer role) was to practise using open questions only, to enable the 'issue holder' to develop his or her own thinking about the issue. One manager asked one open question, 'What is your problem?' and then proceeded to push his own opinions, views and solutions with 14 closed questions!

There are four key reasons for the over-use and inappropriate use of closed questions.

education

As soon as we go to school we are discouraged from using the whats, whys and hows that enable us to grow and learn. Teachers tend not to react well to our probing questions, like 'Why did you do that, Miss?' and our schooling is much more about finding answers – being provided with information from which we develop conclusions – than it is about promoting discovery. As a result, over the years we use more and more closed questions and fewer and fewer open ones.

psychology

One great advantage of closed questions is that there are immediate answers. We know subconsciously that by asking a closed question, we are guaranteeing we will have an answer. This means that outcomes are certain and controlled. Most of us like to be in control, and even if we don't, we like a degree of certainty. With open questions there is an unpredictability of outcomes, generating uncertainty, and we could lose control of the conversation.

Note that this is a perception and not a reality. An effective questioner and listener will be able to control both the direction and flow of any conversation.

ignorance

Few of us are taught about open questions and know how to structure the right sequence in the right way to produce the outcomes we want to achieve. Let us analyse the second, effective conversation above, prefacing the analysis with each question.

1. *'Am I correct?'* All the facts are out in the open to start with, and agreement is gained by S.
2. *'Tell me, why were you late?'* The obvious logical 'why' question. We have to be careful with how we ask the 'why' question. Typically we let ourselves down by the curtness of the wording, with tone of voice and body language that lead to a perception gap. It is taken as implied criticism and results in defensiveness by the follower. This is why B prefaced the 'why' with 'tell me', and would have needed to adopt a tone of voice and consistent body language that conveyed a genuine interest in finding out the reason and not a desire to criticise.
3. *'So what's the problem?'* The hallmark of a good questioner is to demonstrate persistence and jump to valid conclusions. B recognised that the answer given by S was flannel, but rather than repeat the same 'why' question, reached the conclusion that there must be a reason for this atypical behaviour, and so asked the more empathetic question.
4. B is listening and receives a reply, 'My mother is very poorly', which is not an answer. However, he pauses to build the empathy by acknowledging the emotional overtones with the implied closed question. *'It must be very tough for you (is it not?)'.*
5. *'But I don't see why you are late.'* B continues to be persistent – tough but tender. The combination of asking the right question in the right way leads to the answer – it all pours out.
6. *'When do you leave to go home?'* A seemingly innocuous but powerful question. B is not assuming via a closed question that S has cut his working hours,

but gently probing to establish the position. S realises the implication of leaving at the normal time – but comes up with the cut in lunchtime to justify it without any accusation being made.

S is left with the view that his boss is an understanding, empathetic leader – and his motivation and loyalty have been enhanced.

time
Closed questions save time and we are very busy – hence the need to recognise those situations where we need to invest the time to use open questions as appropriate, and those situations where we deliberately use closed questions to avoid investing the time.

key requirements to become an effective questioner

To conclude this section we look at the key requirements to become an effective questioner. The context is a meeting we have planned, which could be for development or performance review or some specific issue (as in the B and S case) that needs to be addressed.

think first
With the time and place known in advance, the more we think and plan the conversation, the more effective it will be. Additionally, during the meeting, use the 'assertive pause' to ensure you remain in control of yourself and hence the questions you ask.

think open question
Because of our tendency to think in terms of closed questions

that make assumptions, we need to think in terms of using an open question. For instance, when recapping, we should not summarise and then ask the closed question, 'Am I right?' Instead, ask, 'What have I omitted?' In the former case, the follower will simply say, 'Yes, you are' even if you have omitted something vital, as they may not want to cause loss of face to their boss. In the latter, they will be much more inclined to advise an omission. The assumption we convey with the closed question is that we have got it right, whereas with the open question, we are deliberately making the point that we are fallible and may have missed something out.

Another powerful example is when we give a briefing to an individual or a team. We tend to say at the end, 'Has everyone understood?', to which the chorus goes up, 'Yes, boss.' We then discover when the team members carry out our brief that they have not understood, but have not dared to display their ignorance or lack of attention to their boss or in front of their peers. However, if we ask someone to summarise – 'To ensure that we all fully understand the brief, do you mind recapping?' – then any gaps in understanding will be identified and can be eliminated. The implementation will be more successful, as it is based on a shared understanding that has been made explicit.

Additionally, when establishing facts, if there is a possibility that the facts are unclear or could be disputed, it is better to go an open question route. Rather than stating the facts and asking, 'Do you agree? it is better to start with, 'Let us establish what are the facts,' and when all the evidence has been brought into play, continue with, 'And let us think of any information we may have overlooked', before getting the closed agreement.

avoid leading questions
Leading questions can be phrased in a closed or open style, and are the antithesis to promoting discovery or even problem solving as they push or lead to the 'one right' answer.

> The chairman thinks we should sack Jones. What do you think? (not very
> open!)
>   Surely you do not have any doubts about our new mission?

A variation is the loaded question. With a leading question, our
own views are implicit. In a loaded question, they are explicit
or loaded in.

> Do you not agree that John has poor time-keeping?
> Why don't you drop dead? (again not a very open question)

avoid 'logical' closed alternatives

Let us say the issue under discussion is a drop in sales.

> Clearly we have to either reduce costs or increase revenue. Which do
> you favour?

Far, far better to go the open route:

> Let us consider all the options we could take to reverse this trend.

Incidentally, 'or' can be used exclusively, as in the above case
(although there is no reason why you could not do both) or
conjunctively: that is, both alternatives can be selected. This
should also be avoided.

> Did you go to the cinema or the theatre?
> Yes!

I do have a caveat to this avoidance of logically closed alternatives. As the Romans said, 'quae cum ita essent' or 'circumstances alter cases'. Young children from a very early age
dislike being simply told what to do. However, for many happy
years, they will succumb to the restricted choice of logically
closed alternatives: 'Either you stop shouting now or I will send
you upstairs!'

use perceptive probing questions

A perceptive probing question is one that you can only ask when you have become a good listener. When you ask good open questions in an empathetic way, the other person opens up – that is their purpose. In the course of answering the particular question, they almost invariably drop in a phrase or even sentence that is significant. This is inevitable as you are getting them to think – either to reveal what was hidden from you, or to reveal what was latent or subconscious (hidden from them), or come up with completely new thoughts. If you are listening acutely, you can easily pick up this phrase, as there will be a slight change in tone of voice or even body language.

Let us take the example of the manager who asked one open, followed by 14 closed questions of the 'issue holder'. The problem as originally stated was that the 'issue holder' was the boss of a number of teams, each of which had a team leader, one of whom had resigned. The boss had complete autonomy as to what action to take, and had to decide whether to hire in a new team leader, promote from within the existing team (in effect downsizing), or promote from within and hire a new team member.

First of all, this manager over-stressed the word 'autonomy'. No one in business has complete autonomy these days, and the problem holder had a boss, who would have some views that needed to be ascertained, but that was not brought up.

Next, although the questioner asked all these closed questions, in this group the issue holder responded as if they were open, because he was so anxious to air this real, important, work-related problem. On three occasions he dropped little clues, which were left unprobed. On the first occasion he referred during a series of statements to the fact he would have a 'bigger job', which should have been picked up and probed, perhaps by, 'That's interesting. I noticed you mentioned that you would be taking on a bigger job. In what ways will your job become bigger?'

On the second occasion, the problem holder dropped in the phrase 'moving away', which should have led to three open questions: 'Thanks for that. You mentioned that you would be moving away. Where will you be going?' After the reply this could have been followed with, 'When will you be going?' and after that reply, 'And what will be the impact on your teams?'

Funnily enough, the third occasion was the *cri de coeur*. The problem holder referred in the midst of other issues and points to 'how he could keep his staff motivated'. The real problem, subsequently uncovered with effective questioning, was, 'How do I keep my teams motivated, when I am going to take on additional responsibilities and be physically separate from them?'

use the right wording

The way the question is worded will have a major impact on the answer. The general rule is to focus the question so as to focus the other person. Some examples are:

'What do you mean precisely?' is better than 'What do you mean?', which could lead to, 'I mean what I say.'

'In what ways is the job bigger?' is better than 'How much bigger is the job?' which could lead to, 'Much, much bigger!'

'What are all the possible actions we can take to reduce absenteeism?' is better than 'How do we reduce absenteeism?', and 'What could all the possible reasons be for sales falling?' is better than 'Why have sales fallen?' Both the former increase the probability of a wider spectrum of ideas.

keep questions simple

On a video, we have a persuasion role play between two managers, where one took more than 10 minutes to ask his question. You should have seen the body language of the listener! If we are not confident, or we are too involved, or we are too rushed and speak before we think, we can get lost. We can start a question, go on a gentle ramble or lecture tour, recover, and revert back to the question in hand. This is to be avoided, as it makes us look silly, and puts the listener to sleep! We must keep our questions simple and to the point.

keep questions single

A golden rule of effective questioning is 'one at a time'. More than one question can lead to confusion or evasion. The respondent can select which one to answer, and the other one or ones can be lost in the subsequent discussion.

A classic example of this occurred a few years ago, when an opposition Member of Parliament in the United Kingdom put forward written questions, intended to embarrass the government by showing the extent of sex discrimination in the Civil Service. Not only did he ask multiple questions, but he ended by asking whether male staff or female staff were in the majority. The junior minister's written reply to the entire set of questions was one word, 'Yes' (deliberately answering the last question, and assuming it had been asked conjunctively).

provide answers when asked

There can be a danger that we get into an exclusive open question mind-set, and always end up answering a question with a question. Sharing your experience and giving your opinions is a vital part of a leadership role. As we know, followers can lack confidence, and need guidance and support. The trick is to try to build up confidence, promote discovery, develop thinking – shift the problem monkey back on the shoulders where it should rightly rest – by asking all the right open questions. However, if and when you are asked for your opinion or your experience, then freely give it. The point is not to impose it early on – to pull first, and push later (if asked).

Too often, we simply push with all those closed, leading, logical alternative questions, and there is no real dialogue – no discovery and relationship enhancement.

practise

Being an effective questioner (and listener) does not come naturally to most. The only way you will improve is to practise, practise, practise, practise and then practise again.

improving staff performance

In this chapter we look at the key requirements to improve the performance of your direct reports. Specifically we look at:

- developing clarity of role;
- setting standards and performance measures;
- giving praise;
- giving constructive criticism;
- coaching and mentoring;
- using appraisals to create learning and growth;
- motivating staff.

developing clarity of role

I have met many, many managers where lack of clarity of their role has caused enormous stress. They can find they are doing work they should not be doing, duplicating others' work or having someone else doing part of the job for which they are responsible and accountable. One particular case that sticks in my mind was an individual who had been hired to be marketing director when his predecessor had been appointed managing director. The managing director, for understandable reasons in terms of staying within his comfort zone, made the marketing director's life a complete misery by giving endless unsolicited advice and keeping under his direct control those aspects of his former role he enjoyed.

If you are responsible for a team of managers or employees, the best approach to this problem is to agree collectively the individual role. However, as individuals are typically hired for specific jobs with specific job descriptions, clarifying the role on an individual basis is also required.

Job descriptions tend not to be helpful, as they often list many qualities that cannot easily be assessed, have a lot of detail about role and responsibilities rather than key areas for action and actions required, and occasionally ask for attributes that are mutually exclusive, such as 'must be a decisive leader … and a team player'. The best way to develop an action-oriented job description, which gives clarity, is to use a 'structured' thinking approach as we did with leadership. For example:

Situation: J is appointed to a new role.
Complication: J is not clear about her role.
Question: what should J do?
Answer: agree an action-oriented job description.
Question: what are the core actions J should carry out?
Keyline answer:

- ■ delight clients;
- ■ generate new business;
- ■ build an effective team;
- ■ develop herself;
- ■ manage her staff.

Level 2 question (generic in this case): How?
Taking 'delight her clients' as an example, a process answer is:

- agree needs;
- meet needs;
- provide after-sales care;
- develop long-term partnerships.

Each of these leads to a lower-level 'How?' For example, under 'agree needs' we could have:

- understand business/cultural context;
- develop empathy;
- ensure own expertise recognised;
- develop thinking;
- demonstrate value to be added;
- agree standards.

At the end of this process, each jobholder has a precise idea of the specific actions required to carry out his or her role successfully. It gives a template for effective time management. Any activity in the list is important and worth spending time on, and any activity that is not part of the revised job description is unimportant and worth spending little or no time on at all.

setting standards and performance measures

We start with a case study

case study

A manager – we can call her Julie – attended a two-module development programme. We had looked at the need to praise when a direct report had met a standard for the first time (praising is covered in the next section). Julie mentioned that she had a direct report who was very competent, but she could never praise him, as her standards were so high. I asked her to provide an example. She said she had developed a very effective project management methodology, and her direct report simply had not managed his projects to her standard. I then innocently asked her if she had advised her direct report of this very effective methodology. Julie said 'No.'

The start of the second module was a review of the personal development plan completed in the first. Julie was delighted to advise that her direct report had now met all her high standards, had been praised regularly, and their working relationship had been transformed.

Performance cannot be measured unless there are standards agreed against which it can be benchmarked. There will be many generic standards such as timeliness, behavioural standards and dress standards, as well as work standards. If any have not been set (and agreed at the time of the job interview), then you, like Julie, need to set them initially. This can be done through the delegation process already covered in Chapter 4. Initially, using the S1 leadership style, the detailed 'how' is when you set the standards. As your followers get more confident and you share the 'how' under the S2 'coaching' style, you are agreeing standards.

These performance measures are concerned with how jobholders carry out their roles on a day-to-day basis. The other performance measures are the SMART objectives to be agreed in all the core action areas:

■ Specific;
■ Measurable;
■ Agreed;
■ Realistic;
■ Timed.

I mention the need to set them in all core action areas, as many organisations focus purely on hard business objectives: for example the senior associate who has to achieve 1600 billable hours in a law firm, or the consultant who has to achieve 70 per cent profitable utilisation, or the salesperson who has to sell £300,000 worth of business. Our behaviour tends to follow our reward systems. Reward systems tend to focus on hard business measures. So we tend to focus all our energies on achieving these hard targets on which promotion and/or bonuses depend. The fact that we do our jobs the best and perform the best and get the best results if we operate in *all* the key areas of our work is lost on us and the organizations we serve.

We can always create reasonably useful qualitative measures of success in any core action area. For instance, if we have to delight internal or external clients, we can carry out client satisfaction surveys with an overall satisfaction rating. If that were to come out first time at 70 per cent, then we can set a SMART objective. Within one year, the overall satisfaction rating will have moved from 70 per cent to 90 per cent (and we can also set interim milestones or measures if we want to measure progress).

giving praise

Giving praise in the right way for the right reason at the right time is generally an underdeveloped and under-utilised skill. Too often we forget to praise, as we are too busy ourselves or we operate in cultures where criticism is the cultural norm. Too often we praise in vague and unhelpful ways such as 'You're a star,' and too often we praise before dumping! Here we look at the three key issues: why praise, when to praise and how to praise.

why praise

The fundamental reason for giving praise is to acknowledge good performance and so encourage the continuance of that good performance. When done effectively, it takes less than a minute and is time very well spent.

when to praise

There are three occasions when praise should be given:

■ *Work meets a standard for the first time.* As you know, standards are set when some one is new to the role, and when you first delegate using the S1 leadership style. By taking the time, in the first instance, to:
- advise the 'what';
- advise the 'why';
- provide a detailed 'how' and set the standards for the specific job being delegated;
- confirm understanding through an open question;
- monitor and review;
- confirm availability and the 'bring me solutions' suggestion;

you are guaranteeing that your direct report will meet the standards and so can be given praise. This starts the relationship off on a virtuous circle where mutual respect is created.

■ *Work exceeds an agreed standard.* Praising those who outperform encourages them to continue.

■ *Work is satisfactory over a long period of time.* For every star there are solid performers, often supporting the stars, who keep up the required standards over a long period of time. They can become neglected and feel unloved, so praising them monthly or bi-monthly pays enormous dividends.

how to give praise

Here is a time sequence of activities with an example.

1   Start by scoping the performance you want to praise. *'Anne, I'd like to talk to you about the report you've prepared over the past three weeks.'*

2. Quote a specific example (or examples) of the individual's performance. *'I'm impressed with the fact that you placed the recommendations at the front of the report so I could see immediately the decisions we need to take.'*

3. Mention personal qualities. *'I also noticed that you've put in a lot of extra hours to meet the deadline, and that you were persistent in getting information from managers who weren't particularly forthcoming.'*

4. Comment on how this benefits the achievement of the team's overall objectives. *'The report is going to be used as part of our decision making at the executive meeting next week.'*

This is short, to the point, and highlights the specific qualities and skills you want to be maintained. Moreover, by providing the necessary detail to praise for good performance, you are showing interest in the direct report, which is also highly motivational. Those leaders who praise on the 'You're a star' basis don't realise that the lack of specifics means that they have not observed and are not showing real interest. This form of praise, especially if repetitive, demotivates.

Before moving on to constructive criticism, how we receive praise affects whether we get praise in the future. Those who say 'It was nothing' or 'It was mainly someone else' will find they do not get much praise again. The simplest way to receive praise is to say 'Thanks.'

giving constructive criticism

As we know, when we receive criticism where the 'intention' is to be constructive, the manifestation of that intention or the environment in which the intention is manifested means we feel simply criticised, which impacts on our self-esteem and makes us angry and defensive. I do not know of any people who go home with a song in their heart and a smile on their faces to say to their loved ones, 'It has been a fantastic day today. I have received masses and masses of constructive criticism.'

Before we give constructive criticism, we should recognise five things:

■ Art critics can give rave reviews – so we should mention the positives as well as the negatives.
■ The time to criticise is when performance has dropped below an agreed standard.
■ The sole objective is raise the performance back to that standard, so we need to have calmed down and got into a positive frame of mind before the discussion.
■ We need to do it in a way that does not erode self-esteem or confidence.
■ We need to recognise that the way we have led the individual may have contributed to his or her poor performance, and be prepared to acknowledge that reality.

I set out a suggested process with an example.

1. Start by scoping the performance you need to criticise. *'Anne, I need to talk to you about your handling of the meeting this morning.'*
2. Praise any good aspects of the performance. *'You kept a really tight rein on the meeting and ensured that everything on the agenda was covered.'*
3. Specify your concerns. *'One area that concerned me was the lack of contribution from some of the quieter members of the team.'*

4. Ask for suggestions. *'If you had to run that meeting again, what could you do to make sure that you keep control and get more input from the quieter members?'*
5. Make your own suggestions. This may or may not be necessary, depending on the response to point 4. There may be an opportunity to build on an idea that the follower has suggested in his or her response.
6. Agree on the action to take. *'OK, so at next week's meeting you'll allow more time for people to respond, and if necessary ask people directly for a contribution.'*
7. Follow up. *'Let's have a brief chat after next week's meeting and see how you feel it's gone.'*

key points

■ After praising, do not put a 'but' or a 'however' in, as when we do that, the person knows that criticism is round the corner and all the preceding positives are instantly erased from memory.

■ Notice the use of the word 'concern' which is a nice euphemism for 'criticism'.

■ The use of the first person 'me' is very effective. Avoid the use of 'we' or 'the team' or a named individual, as it is your personal concern.

■ Bring all the evidence of the poor performance with you, just in case there is denial.

■ Moving straight into asking for suggestions is a very powerful approach for two reasons. First, it avoids rubbing the person's nose in the poor performance. Most managers or staff I have met know when they have done something badly, are kicking themselves and are keen to improve. Second, this is a 'coaching' question. People are much more likely to commit to actions they have put forward or discovered for themselves, rather than those imposed (suggested) by the leader.

coaching and mentoring

In this section we look at:

- what coaching is;
- what its benefits are;
- what qualities a coach needs to have;
- how to coach and mentor.

what coaching is

Coaching is unlocking a person's potential to maximise their own performance. It is helping them to learn rather than teaching them.

(Timothy Gallwey, Harvard educationalist and tennis expert)

Good coaching, and for that matter, good mentoring, should take the performer beyond the limitations of the coach or mentor's own knowledge.

(Sir John Whitmore, *Coaching for Performance*)

the benefits of coaching

The benefits of coaching as opposed to instruction, to the manager, the managed and the organisation that develops a coaching culture, are:

- improved performance and productivity;
- staff development;
- improved learning;
- improved relationships;
- improved quality of life in the workplace;
- more time for the manager;
- more creative ideas;
- better use of people, skills and resources;
- faster and more effective emergency response;
- greater flexibility and adaptability to change.

the qualities a coach needs to have

To be effective, a coach needs to be patient, detached, supportive, interested, perceptive, a good listener, aware, self-aware, attentive and retentive: in short, a COGAL!

> A coach does not need to have experience or technical knowledge in the area in which he or she is coaching, if the coach is truly acting as a detached awareness raiser.
>
> (Sir John Whitmore)

how to coach and mentor

The fundamental purpose of coaching is to raise the awareness of the person being coached and increase motivation to take responsibility – to build a winning mind. This is achieved by the use of open questions that begin broad, and increasingly focus on the detail to maintain the interest of the learner. In determining what aspects of an issue are important, the principle is that questions should follow the interest and train of thought of the learner, not the coach.

Paradoxically, it may also be valuable for the coach to focus upon any aspect that the person being coached appears to be avoiding. To do this in a way that is not perceived as critical, start with a statement followed by a question. 'I notice that you have not mentioned…. Is there a particular reason for this?'

One very popular and effective methodology is to group the sequence of open questions under four headings – the GROW model:

- ▓ Agreeing the **goal** for the session as well as short and long-term objectives.
- ▓ Checking **reality** to explore the current situation.
- ▓ Determining **options** and alternative strategies or courses of action.
- ▓ Agreeing **what** is to be done, **when**, by **whom** and creating the **will** to do it.

CREATOR OR
GROWTH + LEARNING

Coaching is directly concerned with the immediate improvement of performance and development of skills. Mentoring is always one step removed, and is concerned with longer-term acquisition of skills in a developing career by a form of advising and counselling. Whether we label it coaching, advising, counselling or mentoring, if it is done well, the underlying principle and methodology remain the same.

COGALs are fantastic coaches and fantastic coaches are COGALs.

using appraisals to create learning and growth

The annual appraisal (better termed 'performance review') meeting should contain no surprises, as there should be regular reviews of performance either quarterly or when a major project has been completed. Its focus should be on producing a development plan for the coming year, so that performance, growth and learning are maximised.

To ensure that any performance review achieves its objectives, the two principles to be adopted are 'leadership by example' and 'promoting discovery' (or coaching):

As you know, the objective of this meeting is to review your performance and agree a development plan that will result in improved performance. However, to start with, as I am your line manager, I would like us to agree where I have made a positive contribution to your performance, as well as areas where I personally could have managed better.

Where I feel I have had a positive impact is in the areas of ...

Examples I can provide are ...

What do you think?

Where I feel I could have been more effective is the area of ...

Examples are ...

What do think?

I think that to be a better manager this year, I need to commit to ...

Now over to you, Chris. Where do you think you performed well this year? What examples can you provide? What can we do to ensure that next year you spend more time playing to your strengths and improving those areas of excellence?

Turning now to development areas, what areas do you think you would like support?

What examples can you provide? What specifically should we do to ensure a marked improvement in the areas we have agreed?

motivating staff

What motivates us is determined by a combination of what we need and what we value.

motivators and needs

Lower-level needs consist of:

Psychological: self-preservation, basic survival needs.
Safety: protection from threat, security, steady job, basic fringe benefits (health insurance, pensions).

Higher-level needs consist of:

Social: acceptance by others, affiliation, belonging, equity/ justice for one's groups.
Esteem: self-respect, confidence, achievement., autonomy, reputation, recognition, respect and appreciation.
Self-fulfilment: realisation of potential, creativity, continuous development.

Research by Herzberg indicated that the lower-level needs, or hygiene factors – the context of the job – are dissatisfiers, not true motivators. So if the roof of your building blew off, that would cause extreme dissatisfaction and until it was replaced, you would be demotivated. However, if you enjoyed a staff restaurant and they added a wider range of dishes, that would not motivate you to work harder.

motivators and values

Although higher-level needs – the job content – are motivators, the degree to which an individual is motivated by each need is determined by his or her values. If one value is dominant, then that leads to a specific personality type or orientation. There are four basic orientations:

▪ *Safety orientation:* a creature of habit, likes everything to be under control, dislikes change, unadventurous in dress and appearance, unambitious, socially retiring.

▪ *Affiliation orientation:* actively seeks the company of other people, is eager to interact and make friends, likes to be liked, often non-assertive and warm, may talk at length about family, friends, outside interests.

▪ *Influence orientation (recognition, power, esteem):* tends to be firm, direct and competitive, likes to be persuasive in dealings with people, active in the politics of the organisation, knows who is who and develops ways of convincing others to accept his or her ideas, may express status through symbols, likes to impress, to act as a representative of people and to give advice.

▪ *Achievement orientation (self-fulfilment, creativity):* likes to work alone, enjoys realistic challenges and getting things done, sets clear precise goals, does not work well under close supervision, endless striving to realise goals, likes to initiate rather than imitate, demands very high standards from others, and searches for opportunities for creativity.

The implications for leaders are to:

▓ Focus on job content as generic motivators for the job-holder.

▓ Recognise what individual orientations are, and be flexible so that the job matches the orientation. (Recognition can be obtained by simply asking the job-holder.)

▓ Drive themselves and their teams towards achieving the organisational culture/values, which typically are achievement-oriented, sometimes with aspects of affil-iation.

To conclude this section and the chapter, we look at a list of things you should do to motivate your staff, from the most important to the least important. These are research findings from asking followers what their leaders should do to motivate them, and then getting them to prioritise. When I studied the list, I realised that almost without exception, these actions were absent or very weak in most current cultures. We seek motiva-tion where it is lacking.

1 provide effective feedback

This is generally not provided. It certainly is not provided by the annual downward appraisal, which both parties tend to dread, and so defer for as long as possible. Leaders with S1 domination tell their direct reports where they are weak, leaders with S2 domination tell the followers where they are strong and weak, leaders with S3 domination simply praise and tell their direct reports they are brilliant to avoid a demotiva-tional backlash, and leaders with S4 domination just accept whatever the follower says.

Receiving effective feedback is highly motivational, as it enables us to develop and grow so that we do our jobs better, have a greater sense of achievement, and can walk along the path to more challenging and stimulating work.

2 provide supportive leadership/adapt your leadership styles

The first arises from the excess of S1 – us acting too much as bosses. The second from the inflexibility of leadership styles demonstrated. Leaders become comfortable with a given style or style combination.

3 delegate

I think it is ironic that so many leaders are stressed out of their minds because they will not delegate. There is a combination of different reasons:

■ perceived lack of time;
■ belief that they are the most competent to do the job;
■ lack of faith in the follower;
■ fear that if they delegate away their jobs, they will have no jobs to keep.

Yet followers are crying out for more challenging and stimulating work so that they can take on more responsibility, achieve more, and develop and grow. When leaders recognise that any follower has the potential to improve, and that effective delegation is a process that needs to be planned, and not a simple act of dumping, then stress reduces significantly for all parties involved. Equally, when successful, leaders will be praised for running such a splendid ship, and be able to make a greater contribution to the strategic end of their role.

4 allow risk-taking

Taking risks is a prerequisite to learning, and learning is necessary in a world of change – change being defined as 'making or becoming different'. Most cultures blame mistakes, and discourage risk-taking. The key to success is to manage risks. Through effective coaching and review processes, it can be agreed what risks can be taken, and parameters can be set, avoiding the consequences of just letting go (S4) or keeping total control (S1)

5 train and develop

While many organisations are introducing formal training and development programmes and personal development plans at the back-end of the appraisal process, many are not. Moreover the training and development process has to be effective. We in the training world use the jargon 'user chooser'.

Where the employee determines and chooses, the process is much more effective than when he or she is sent on remedial therapy, or where the development plans have been told or sold, but not discovered. Additionally, many training establishments rely too heavily on lecturing, not knowing that it is not the way we learn. Indeed research carried out by the UK Post Office and IBM (UK) proves that if we are lectured at, we remember 70 per cent after three days and a miserly 10 per cent after three months (and after a few years, I would suggest hardly anything at all). However if input is supported by explanation and then we are tested (preferably in small effective study groups), and then there is shared review of results/experience to produce short-cuts or new knowledge, our memory after three days soars above 85 per cent and after three months is above 70 per cent.

6 generate high expectations

In one company once, the CEO decided that the staff should set their own targets, and not have them mandated or set for them. The managers were very dubious about this (but of course, had to go along with it) as they assumed the employees would be lazy – set themselves low, easily achievable targets. Much to their surprise they found the reverse happened, and they had to try to persuade their staff to reduce their targets, which they felt were so high they would not be achieved (which would demotivate).

7 provide goals

As we know, written goals and well-formed outcomes are key to high performance.

8 acknowledge achievement

A word of praise has more motivational power than a thousand words of blame.

building an effective team

In this chapter, we look at:

- why build a team;
- what the right range is;
- what an effective team looks like;
- how teams develop;
- how to build an effective team.

why build a team?

The reasons are simple. An effective team is the most powerful way to develop the individual and to maximise business performance. As Anthony Montebello and Victor Buzzotta said, 'Companies that are willing to rethink old ways and develop teams can profit by increasing quality and productivity. And they can develop a work-force that is motivated and committed.' Tom Peters says: 'I observe that the power of the team is so great that it is often wise to violate common sense and force a team structure on almost anything ... companies that do will achieve a greater focus, stronger task orientation, more innovation and enhanced individual commitment.'

Research by the American Society of Training and Development found that those companies that developed a team approach saw productivity, quality, customer and job satisfaction improve, and an increased ability of team members to resolve their own disputes. Finally, the research findings reported by A J Romiszowksi in his book *Producing Instructional Systems* were that an effective team enabled each individual to become more intelligent, creative, and sociable as well as a more rounded personality.

the right range

I once talked to the managing director of a multinational travel services company. During the course of our conversation, he stated that he had a fantastic team. I then asked him how many were in his team, to which came the reply 10,000!

The range of numbers that enable an effective team to be produced is from four to seven. The lower limit of four is because there is a requirement of critical mass to enable the beneficial outcomes for the individual. The higher limit is seven because when an individual is part of an effective or high-performing team, she or he becomes very confident and very self-aware, as his or her individual needs have been met. As a result that person can focus on the other members of the team, and demonstrate a high level of awareness of what each other member is thinking and feeling. There is a limit to how many people we can accommodate at the same time. Additionally, when we start building a team, at various stages it is critically important that everyone is involved and everyone contributes.

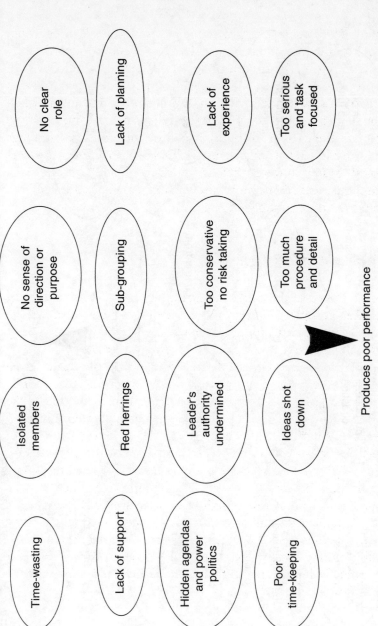

Figure 7.1 *The ineffective team*

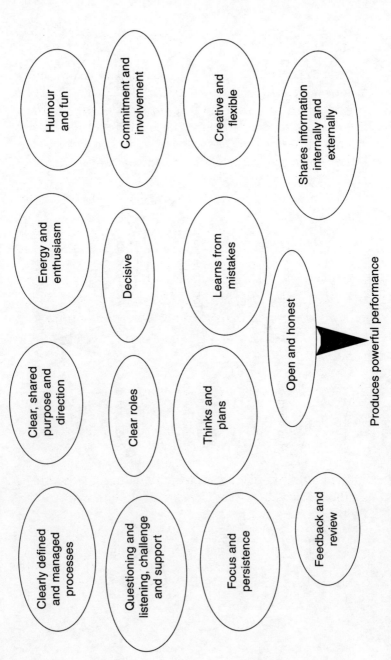

Figure 7.2 *The effective team*

what an effective team looks like

If you are going to build an effective team, you need to know what it looks like. This is a very easy thing to do. I would ask you to grab paper and pencil, think back to all the meetings you have been to in your working life, and list all the factors that demotivated you – that made you wish you were somewhere else. Once you have done that, then reverse all these negatives to produce the positives. You will find that you have painted a picture of an effective team – and a wonderful picture it is.

When a team is operating effectively, what it has achieved is synergy. The literal meaning from the ancient Greek is 'working together'. More specifically, it means that the creative output of the group is greater than the sum of what each individual could produce if thinking alone, and the quality of the decision making is better than any individual could produce, if deciding alone.

how teams develop

All teams go through certain stages from the moment of formation to the moment of effective performance. The stages are linked to development levels, because a team can be considered as an individual entity that passes from immaturity to maturity through the careful and effective deployment of knowledge and skills by the coordinator.

Figure 7.3 sets out the stages, differentiating between the four – confusion, conflict, cooperation and commitment – that are part of a progression and from which the group can easily move, and the two – control and consensus – that can become stable states for considerable periods of time. The key characteristics of each of the progressive phase are set out in Table 7.1.

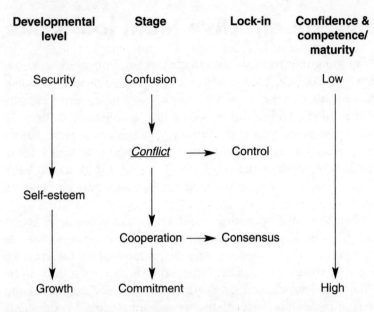

Figure 7.3 *Stages of team development*

Table 7.1

Confusion	Conflict	Cooperation	Commitment
Polite Cautious Impersonal Awkward Reserved Uncertain Insecure	Confrontational Some team members feeling isolated No sense of direction Poor time keeping Demotivated	Getting organised Developing a team identity Developing skills and procedures Giving and receiving feedback High task orientation Confronting issues	Closeness Group maturity Resourceful and flexible Effective Supportive Open and sharing Tolerant

Key points are:

- ■ The 'lock-in' state control occurs when there is a very dominant leader, whom all the team members willingly follow and obey. There is no synergy. Such leaders are usually larger than life, charismatic, with strong personalities and therefore have a tendency to want to control. A lock-in state can quite often occur at times such as the initial stage of confusion, when team members have a high degree of insecurity and a need for direction and guidance. They are therefore vulnerable to manipulation and control.

- ■ The 'lock-in' state consensus is where there is no leader or an ineffective coordinator. The group, typically, is a peer group that has bonded very well, but there is no focus nor drive to task completion. There is no synergy.

- ■ The path to the commitment level can be very rapid when the leader acts as a coordinator and focuses initially on creating the team vision and values, and gaining the individual commitment to attitudes and actions that a commitment-level team exhibits. Effective coordination will bypass the 'conflict' stage. One senior executive, demonstrating how 'a little knowledge is a dangerous thing', deliberately created the conflict stage – 'blood on the carpet' – but failed to achieve 'commitment', just resignations.

- ■ For many teams in the workplace, the conflict stage can represent the state they are in most of the time (which is why it is in italics and underlined in Figure 7.3). This is because there is no coordination and the leader is either weak or strong, but with insufficient personality and charisma to control some of the team members. This reality explains why team members are demotivated, as they gain no value and precious time is wasted.

- ■ Teams will inevitably degenerate into the conflict stage with any significant or sudden change.

Table 7.2

Change	What stage team reverts to	Strategies required by team leader
Unexpected	Conflict	Review meeting Focus on problem solving
Varying team membership	Cooperation then conflict	Attendance rule Two-way communication with missing team members
Permanent departure of a team member	Cooperation then conflict	Review meeting New task process Re-prioritisation team/individual work Expand areas for team working
Replacement of a team member/ additional team member	Conflict	Back to team building, as if all team were new
Task completed new task	Conflict	New task process

Table 7.2 sets out the nature of the change, the impact on the team, and the strategic response required by the team leader.

how to build an effective team

The key requirements to ensure that you can build an effective team are as follows.

believe in yourself

Only when we are confident in our own abilities, have developed our self-esteem and become at ease with ourselves will we have the capability to focus externally and build others – exactly the same attitude as is required to be an effective leader of an individual direct report.

believe in your team-members

In an experiment some time ago, a group of 'average ability' young schoolchildren were split into three groups and each group taught by a different teacher. None of the children had met the teachers before. Let us call the teachers A, B and C. The A teacher was told she was receiving bright, able, committed children, the B teacher told she was receiving average, run-of-the-mill kids, and the C teacher a bunch of below average, rude and rebellious kids. Six months later each of the three groups was performing and behaving exactly according to the expectations given to each teacher.

If we have faith in the potential of all our team members, suspend our initial judgements and rigorously avoid the display of any favouritism, all team members will have confidence in themselves and you will be able to create an effective team.

use the group discovery technique (GDT)

Application of this technique guarantees creative synergy. Of over 1000 groups I have taught the technique to and applied it with, apart from two individuals in one group, all the other individuals (over 5000) have agreed that they would not have produced as many ideas if they had been thinking on their own, and that GDT improves individual creativity.

Once the issue/problem/opportunity has been identified, there are four requirements to the technique:

1. Separate out the generation of ideas – the exploration phase – from evaluation.
2. No criticism (by word or body language) is allowed during exploration. It is the role of you – the team leader – to ensure this is followed by all, leading by example.
3. Build on other's ideas. Individuals should think of their ideas as gifts to the group, and let the other individuals develop it into full bloom.
4. Question assumptions.

An example of the need to avoid criticism and build on other's ideas is a true story concerning the Alaskan Electricity Company, operating in the 1970s. It supplied electricity via wires carried by overground telegraph poles to the native population, which was scattered over a vast terrain. The weather conditions were so bad that frequently the weight of snow and ice that formed on the wires was so great that the wires snapped, cutting off the electricity supply. The Alaskan Electricity Company had to send teams of workers hundreds if not thousands of miles to repair the wires. When they solved the problem, they were close to bankruptcy, as the costs of repair were spiralling out of control, and there was a limit to the amount the company could charge the indigenous population.

We will run through the suggestions made and answers provided. Please note that the problem was solved by using only open questions, and the suggestions were very logical in nature, which proves that those of us who are very logical can be very creative, provided we suspend judgement and build rather than destroy through criticism.

■ Why not shake the poles?
■ How do we shake the poles?
■ Why not use polar bears?
■ How do we motivate the bears to shake the poles?
■ Why not put meat on top of the poles?
■ How do we get meat on top of the poles?

- Why not use a helicopter?
- Why not forget about the bears and use the whirring blades of the helicopter to get rid of the snow and ice, before it forms?

And this is what they did. The cost of prevention was much lower than the cost of cure. 'Valid' criticism along the lines of 'That is a stupid idea as there are far too many poles to shake', and 'I have done my research and there are only 1000 polar bears, far too few to shake the poles', would have prevented this solution ever being found.

In the context of questioning assumptions, please look at Figure 7.4 for only a few seconds and write down how many squares there are.

When I do this exercise with a combined group of, say, 10 managers, I typically get around six different answers. Answers vary from 1 to 16, 17, 20, 21, 25, 26, 29 and 30. It all depends

How many squares are there?

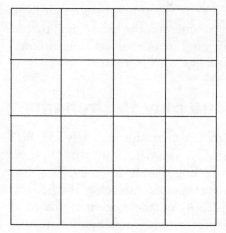

Figure 7.4 *Questioning assumptions*

on the assumptions we make. Different individuals interpret the same information differently, as we all have blind spots and believe that we what see is reality. Instead of a number answer to a silly question, imagine this was for us the one right answer to a real problem or issue. Not much chance of building a team or producing lots of different answers if more than half the group believe their answer is the only one to consider!

When I was given the problem I was initially very smug, as I came up with 30, which I felt sure was the right answer. There is one large 4 × 4 square, 4 squares that are 3 × 3, 9 squares that 2 × 2 and 16 squares that are 1 × 1. This produces a total of 30. However:

■ There is a square under the '?'.
■ Whenever the 1 × 1 squares intersect, there is a much smaller, partially defined square. These can easily be visualised or 'seen', and there are 20 of those.
■ One a more esoteric note, we all saw the word 'squares'. How many squares did we see, when we saw 'squares'?

Introducing GDT is the single best way to build an effective team, because it generates the behaviours that are the hallmark of high-performing teams: good questioning and listening skills, and challenge with support.

identify and play to strengths

This is vital to build confidence early on. Professor Drucker once said that there is a defect in many Western cultures when it comes to selecting people for jobs. There is a tendency to focus on any weaknesses and select the person with the least, rather than identifying the key strengths to do the job and selecting the person who matches the profile most closely, ignoring any weaknesses that person may have that will not affect job performance.

Later, when cohesion and confidence has grown, new skills will be developed through effective feedback processes.

meet regularly

If practical, meet once a week – Friday afternoon or Monday morning – to review, share experiences, refocus energies and provide mutual support.

use process

The power of process must not be understated. 'Process' means the predetermined sequence of steps that will produce the best result in any specific work activity, such as:

■ completing a project;
■ completing a task;
■ building a team;
■ coaching a subordinate;
■ completing a marketing plan;
■ improving a relationship.

Given the goal or intention, the process can be uncovered by asking the following questions. In order to achieve this goal:

■ What should be done first, and why?
■ What should be done second, and why?
■ And so on...

Once the process has been developed, an estimation of the time taken to complete each activity in the sequence should be determined. The breakdown of time is, naturally, put into the framework of the external deadline given for completion. If no such deadline exists (as in coaching a subordinate), it is important that you put in as tight a deadline as you consider feasible. The reason is that putting an agreed process in place, and having the discipline to stick to it, generally means the goal will be achieved much more speedily than it can be without process thinking or planning.

An effective 10-step process for completing a team task is:

■ Appoint a coordinator to help the group through the process. (This is necessary for immature groups, and helps even with groups working well, especially for survival in the event of a crisis/unexpected setback.)

■ Clarify the brief, identify and question assumptions. (It is often insufficient challenge and exploration at the start that leads to confusion and poor execution. It may also be possible, in this phase, to produce a smarter objective or find a neat way to solving the problem.)

■ Ensure everyone is clear about and fully understands the brief/objective/task as refined. Remember to get confirmation of understanding through the appropriate open question.

■ Check your resources – what you have available to complete the task: time, equipment and the skills of the individuals in the group.

■ Initiate the group discovery technique (GDT) – avoiding criticism – to generate ideas.

■ Select at least two ideas. (One can be held in reserve as a contingency if the other does not work out in practice.)

■ Develop and plan your first-choice idea, allocating roles: who does what, why, where and when. (This may include the role of 'task manager' – the individual who is best suited to managing the implementation of the plan.)

■ Test it out, and fall back on the contingency plan if necessary. (Depending on resource requirements for the original idea, time can be saved if both ideas are being developed, planned and tested in parallel.)

■ Review.

■ Implement.

develop vision, values and behaviours

It is vital that the team knows what success looks like – develops the vision and values and behaviours for the team, before focusing on the task. Often, leaders have a natural and understandable drive to get the task done, as they are under enormous pressure with many, many projects and tight deadlines and are naturally task-focused. Just as many companies are developing a vision and values for all employees, because these help provide focus and motivate (if done well!), so should you, as leader, ensure they are developed for the team you lead.

One process to achieve this that does not take very long, and which we have partially covered is:

- Ask all the team members (and include yourself) to list all aspects of working in groups that they have disliked/demotivated them and the reasons.
- Develop the collective view and causes.
- Reverse the causes and effects.
- Agree a vision statement that distils the essence of the vision.
- Agree values and behaviours that underpin the vision and will help bring it into being.

The results of this process for one work team were:

Our team, when effective, will have a clear, shared sense of direction and purpose, with enthusiastic, committed team members who are all involved and participate. We will focus on achieving stretching and demanding tasks and goals, supporting and helping each other develop and grow our individual strengths. We will have fun together, and be able to question and challenge each other so that the team and the individual can continuously improve.

The core values, which will help us become an effective team, are openness, honesty, mutual respect, trust, sharing and humour.

The behaviours (our ground rules) that will bring our vision into being are:

- ▓ sharing;
- ▓ creating a safe confidential environment;
- ▓ listening;
- ▓ staying focused and contributing;
- ▓ trying out others' ideas;
- ▓ altering opinions;
- ▓ praising and encouraging;
- ▓ suppressing ego;
- ▓ questioning.

As team leader, your role is to lead by example on the behavioural front and ensure any individual breach is quickly corrected. By going through this process and ensuring the ground rules are followed, you ensure very rapid progression to the commitment level, bypassing the conflict stage completely. This is because the behaviours the team commits to and follows at the beginning are those of an effective team. Do remember that inevitably there will be changes that reduce the team to conflict level, so have the strategies at the forefront of your mind to regain commitment.

promote feedback

It is critically important that feedback only takes place when the team has developed a measure of cohesion. Far, far too many trainers, internal and external consultants and team leaders introduce feedback too early in the team development process.

Many years ago, I attended an in-company team development programme lasting a fortnight. There were three teams, and only the one I was in developed into an effective unit. On the final Thursday afternoon the two tutors told us all to go to our syndicate rooms and write down all the things we liked about each other and disliked about each other, and pass them around the team. I did not like the sound of this at all, and suggested when we got to our syndicate room that we wrote all the positives but only one negative.

We did this, but even so, later in the evening, there was a minor verbal scuffle between two of our team. When we went back to the debriefing session, we decided to play a game on the tutors, and pretended to be psychologically traumatised by the experience. We spent half an hour looking down at our papers, refusing to look at each other or anyone else. In the evening we told the tutors that it was just a joke, but they did not believe us.

However, what happened in another group is the real story. The tutors had rotated the leadership role throughout the programme, and one of the individuals (male) had been a very poor leader. He had been very arrogant, a know-it-all and very 'command and control'. His team members seized the opportunity provided by the tutors to stick it to him with both barrels. He could not handle this, a classic case of the cumulator (remember perception gaps?) in action. He got very drunk, smashed up some furniture and hit a delegate from another programme. He was subsequently sacked.

When each individual in the team is robust enough, because of the cohesion and mutual support that has been created, then the same approach should be taken as with the annual performance review: lead by example and use a coaching approach.

remember your role

Research carried out by TMS (Team Management Systems International) proved that teams that are coordinated are far more effective than teams that are not. COGALs are coordinators of process and not controllers of people. I have used the word 'coordinator' throughout this chapter, and already covered key aspects of the role. To summarise, the effective coordinator:

- ▓ Introduces GDT, and ensures the technique is effectively practised – 'stamps on criticism'.
- ▓ Leads the process to create the vision, values and behaviours, and ensures the behavioural ground rules are followed subsequently.

▨ Leads the development of process to achieve specific goals, and ensures each step is completed in the right sequence within the time allocated; manages the implementation of any agreed process. This can be quite tough. The coordinator role is not an easy option.

▨ Ensures every individual in the group contributes. In unstructured, uncoordinated groups, the extroverts dominate and the introverts stay quiet. This inevitably has a negative impact on team working. At the end of such a meeting, the leader thinks that everyone is in agreement and committed to action; that team spirit is high. A little while later, along comes one of the introverts and puts forward a much better course of action than the one that has been adopted. What does the leader do – tell the rest of the team what the better solution is and ask them to get on with it? If so, the leader will guarantee rapid descent of the team to the conflict level. Alternatively, should the leader squash the better idea, alienating the introvert and denying a better outcome?

▨ Puts coordination ahead of personal contribution. It is better for the creation of team synergy to focus on the coordination role than on making your own contribution. If you put (as most leaders do) your penny in earlier, then the politically correct (and there are always a few of those) will agree with you, and team synergy goes down the plughole. Make it a rule to contribute last, and you may find that you do not have to contribute at all.

Once you have succeeded in building your effective team, you should consider rotating the coordinating role. You will have acted as a very effective role model, and the team members will learn a vital skill for the future.

Finally, promote humour and enjoy yourself. The effective team is the most exhilarating experience we are ever likely to have in the workplace.

leading change

In this final chapter, we look at a key aspect of your leadership – leading change effectively. We start with how you react to sudden change, and from that produce a transition or reaction curve. We then look at how to gain maximum benefit from change, and how we can build commitment to change in those we lead. We conclude by asking you to complete the change preference questionnaire, and explain how you can improve your leadership of change.

how we react to change

Let us start by promoting discovery in you, the reader, rather than simply telling you the answer. I would like you to think back to an occasion when you experienced a change that was sudden, either in its announcement or in the occurrence, and that you perceived negatively. Examples are receiving unexpected criticism in an area in which you thought yourself competent, from someone you trusted and whose opinion you respected; being advised you were being made redundant; being told by a former partner that she or he was finishing the relationship – any change that was sudden, affected you personally and was initially perceived negatively. Unfortunately, there is bound to be some such change in your past.

Once you have recalled the change, take a pen and piece of paper and write down your feelings, thoughts and actions – but separated into three time frames:

Immediate: the instant of the occurrence or announcement.
Short-term: hours and days after.
Long-term: looking back after months or years.

It would be very helpful for you to complete the exercise before carrying on reading, as otherwise there will be no discovery.

When I ask groups of managers to carry out this exercise, they invariably describe what is termed the transition or reaction curve. I imagine you will have done likewise. It is set out in Figure 8.1. I will explain the chart in some detail. We are looking at how we react to sudden negative change, the phases of reaction we go through over time, and considering the impact those phases have on our development level. The assumption is that we are fairly high on the self-esteem level – we have quite a strong belief in our self-worth, our competence and our capability. If you like, we are quite mature.

shock and denial

The first reaction is one of shock. The suddenness, coupled with the lack of continuity, means that there is no connection with our existing mental model of reality. We have had neither prior warning nor expectation of the event. Our reaction is purely instinctive and 'animal'. We are caught like a rabbit in the sudden glare of car headlights, and freeze. We do not believe what we necessarily cannot believe; we deny the actuality that, at that moment in time, has no meaning.

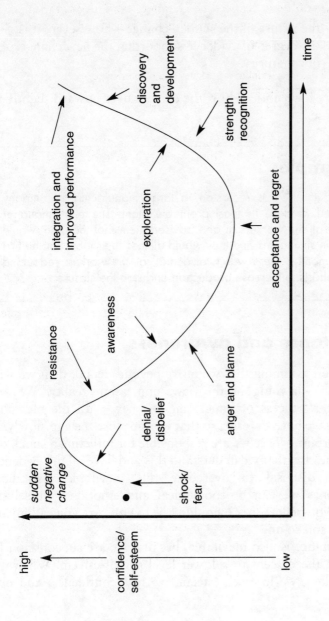

Figure 8.1 *The reaction curve*

This is usually a short-lived phase, but not necessarily so. The key factors at play are:

- the nature of the sudden change – how severe it is;
- the degree of evidence supporting the new change;
- our maturity.

You may have noticed how the curve moves upward slightly in this phase.

---

example

During the 1970s recession, a large manufacturing company decided to close its least profitable plant. The plant manager called all the workers in and advised them that the plant would close in six months and they would all lose their jobs. For the first three months, there was total denial, as the workers redoubled their efforts to increase production and stop the closure.

---

resistance and awareness

However, assuming that we move beyond denial, then we will resist the dawning of the new, unpleasant reality. We are starting a process of integrating the new with the old, and initially we have to resist, so that we can close the gap slowly. It is important, where we are responsible for inflicting a shock on someone else, that we understand this and have all the evidence at our disposal to overcome this inevitable resistance. Sometimes we can be too logical and emotional ourselves. 'Don't you believe me? I wouldn't lie to you. Are you calling me a liar?' and so on.

Resistance is also inevitable, because we are subconsciously fighting the descent to a lower level of self-esteem. When we are sacked, we lose self-esteem, we lose confidence, and our competence declines. We become more insecure. Few seek out that reality.

---

example

A professional was made redundant during the 1990s recession. She was very competent, but the organisation, because of cost cutting necessitated by the recession, decided that her function was no longer required. She was advised clearly of this, but for some time felt that she was incompetent. Evidence played a strong part in overcoming that perception, as the organisation subsequently used her services as an independent consultant, and paid her roughly twice the amount she received when salaried.

---

anger and blame

As our awareness grows that this change represents a new reality, as our resistance is overcome, we stay gripped by emotion. The emotion associated with shock is fear, an inevitable consequence of the high level of uncertainty instantly generated. Now the emotion is one of anger and blame. We 'kick against the pricks', 'rail against fate'. The anger can be both internally and externally focused.

Part of self-blame that can linger into and beyond acceptance is regret. 'If only I had ...' How often do children blame themselves, their perceived incompetence and inadequacy for their parents' divorce? How often does regret for the passing of good times stay with us forever?

A confident extrovert tends to blame others, and gets the balance wrong. A less confident introvert tends to blame himself or herself – and gets the balance wrong.

Blame is a necessary, but fundamentally counter-productive phase, associated with the emotional response. If we are operating at a high level of self-esteem, then the blame phase tends to be temporary and not too intense. This a fundamental point in terms of the shape of the curve. The higher our existing self-esteem, the quicker the transition, and the shallower the dip in terms of loss of confidence and self-esteem. There is unfortunately an element of the virtuous and the vicious in our reactions to sudden negative change. The lower our self-esteem, the more vicious the reaction, and the higher, the more virtuous.

acceptance

Most of us will move eventually – it can be hours, days, weeks, months or years – to acceptance. However the nature of that acceptance and the extent to which it is a temporary phase on a downward or upward path will vary. Recognition of the likely reaction curve is critically important, as it enables us to move from unconscious incompetence (at the mercy of the winds of reaction, we do not recognise) to conscious incompetence (knowing why what is happening is happening), which gives the possibility of our cerebral side intervening positively.

exploration, discovery and integration

Provided the nature of our acceptance has a rational and positive dimension, then we will move into exploration. We have to fight to be rational, to accentuate the positive we do not feel, to seek support, to retain balance, to force out blame and replace it with detached understanding, and thereby preserve as much self-esteem as we can. We must let the heart weep (mourning is vital) but force the head to change the heart.

We are complex creatures. Often we are driven by emotions, and use irrational logic to justify them. We tend to feel before we think. However, if we are prepared to listen, to explore, to open up and out, then the emotion, the intuition will change. Intuition, after all, is the subconscious learning from experience. If we are prepared to expose ourselves to new thoughts, new feelings, new experiences, our learning and our intuition will change.

So the key to the ascent up the growth phase is to explore and evaluate from the base of acceptance, not on our own, but with others; to discover new meaning and develop new skills, to use those hidden strengths that adversity brings closer to the surface, but which we need to consciously uncover and tap into.

Finally, we need to integrate the new learning with the past, which was so suddenly changed. We need to review and reflect – to look back, not in anger but with understanding.

gaining maximum benefit from change

A key point to make at this stage is that if we are involved in the decisions that affect our working lives, and if we involve others in those decisions that affect them, there will be no reaction curve, and the effective management of change. This is one of many reasons why team-based organisations not only have more motivated and profitable staff, but also are more effective in developing and implementing the changes that are required today.

case study

A large insurance company recognised that to survive and grow in rapidly changing market conditions, it would have to change its customer base and distribution channels – two very significant changes. So the board spent six months developing its strategy in considerable detail. It was poised to roll out the strategy when a junior board member asked a key question. 'We know that we have developed the best strategy, but how are we going to moti-vate our senior managers to implement it?'

The response was remarkable, and remarkably effective. The company flew all its senior managers to Copenhagen for three days, split them up into teams, and presented them with the prob-lems and all the research findings – but none of the board strategy.

There were two outcomes. First, the teams all came up with the same strategic response; and second, they were fully motivated to implement it, which they did. This included some of those managers making themselves redundant!

However the consequences of organisational size, existing culture, competitive pressures, and the need for rapid reaction or proaction are that decisions on change are advised to us as leaders suddenly, and we have to pass them downwards.

To conclude this section we look at how you lead yourself through the reaction curve, and how you lead others through it.

how to lead yourself through the reaction curve

case study

I was talking to a group of senior managers about a major change that had been introduced recently in their company. It was a new appraisal and reward system. What they had said to their junior managers was that the system was unfair and divisive, but they would just have to implement it for their staff because that was the way it was.

If we are in the anger and blame phase, we are unable to manage change downwards effectively. We have to have moved ourselves to the 'sunny uplands' before we move others to the same spot. Five actions that will help are:

■ Use the assertive pause to control your emotions.
■ If only the 'what' has been advised, seek out the source of the decision/change to find out the 'why'. Do not challenge the change but simply say, 'It will help me manage the change for my staff if you could share your thinking behind the change.' There are three different outcomes, all of which are beneficial:
  – In the positive environment you have created due to your mature approach, you may be able to change the change. Using the PBA rule you may be able to sell a different and better change.
  – When we fully understand the thinking behind any change, it will often make sense. If we agree, the reaction curve will be avoided.
  – If we don't agree, but cannot change the change, at least understanding will accelerate the path to acceptance.
■ Seek support from a work colleague you can trust, or a partner or friend.
■ Try to visualise the sunny uplands – paint a picture of the change successfully introduced.
■ Focus all the time on all the benefits that any change brings in its wake.

how you lead others

Different individuals with different change preferences and different levels of self-esteem will go through the reaction curve at different rates, with different degrees of intensity. A generic approach to reduce the duration and intensity, when briefing is:

▓ Provide full detail of the change/decisions made, relating it and the reasons for it to any interests and concerns that have been expressed previously by your followers. (Remember the grapevine will have worked overtime, typically exaggerating the negative, which is excellent news when the actuality is much better.)

▓ Share the questions and thought processes involved in reaching the decision.

▓ Demonstrate your enthusiasm and commitment to the change (words, tone of voice and body language), painting your picture of the sunny uplands and all the benefits, and leading by example.

Finally, we look in Table 8.1 at behaviours in each of the four key stages – denial, resistance, exploration, and commitment – and set out strategies to move individuals to the 'sunny uplands'. Note: in the last chapter, we set out the strategies to be used for all the changes that can happen to a team.

Now we turn to considering your change preference, and ask you to complete the change preference questionnaire.

your preference when managing change

For each of the areas covered below, please choose the phrase, word, action and so on with which you identify most. Give that preference 4 marks. In each category there are four choices, so you need to allocate 3 marks to your next choice, then 2, and finally 1 mark for the item with which you least identify.

Let us take the first example, where you imagine that you have total freedom to choose between four different jobs. In this case I have chosen social worker (4 marks), followed by researcher (3 marks) followed by writer (2 marks), with administrator bringing up the rear with the final single point.

Table 8.1

Key stage	Behaviour	Strategies to progress
Denial	Carry on regardless Not talking No interaction Cliques 'It's happened before'	Give information Encourage to talk Include within change system Second them Don't give up
Resistance	Openly aggressive Derogatory comments Impede others Withhold information Sabotage Drag feet	Give them something to do Question to find out reasons Peer group pressure Include in team Be assertive Give them time
Exploration	More positive Open minded Interested Asking open quetions	Give more information Praise Get them involved Ask for ideas Delegate tasks
Commitment	Enthusiastic Motivated Promote change to others	Don't forget them, keep them involved Empower Praise Work with resistors

Jobs

Researcher

Administrator

Writer

Social worker

Marks

A	3
B	1
C	2
D	4

Please complete the form, and carry out the scoring set out in Figure 8.2. Each mark for each set of choices is transferred to one of four categories LD, CC, PF, PC, appropriately labeled: so for the choices made in the example, the C mark of 2 goes in the PC column, the A mark of 3 goes in the LD column and so on. When scoring, find the letter and put the mark corresponding to the letter in the space next to it.

1. Jobs

Marks

Researcher	A
Administrator	B
Writer	C
Social worker	D

2. Words

Marks

Harmony	A
Beauty	B
Intellect	C
Efficiency	D

3. Words

Marks

Keep	A
Evaluate	B
Share	C
Change	D

4. Words   Marks

Idea

Feeling

Organisation

Fact

A	
B	
C	
D	

5. Phrases   Marks

The right answer

Safety first

Go for it

Sixth sense

A	
B	
C	
D	

6. Sayings   Marks

Smile and the whole world smiles

Nothing ventured, nothing gained

The facts speak for themselves

Look before you leap

A	
B	
C	
D	

7. How someone who did not like you might describe you
                                              Marks

Being stuck in the mud

Being as dry as dust

Wearing your heart on your sleeve

Having your head in the clouds

A	
B	
C	
D	

8. Attitude to risk

Do you prefer to:

Marks

Take risks	A
Share risks	B
Avoid risks	C
Analyse risks	D

A	
B	
C	
D	

9. Attitude to change

Do you prefer to:

Marks

Analyse and evaluate ideas	A
Implement ideas that are practical	B
Generate ideas	C
Look to see how ideas will affect others	D

A	
B	
C	
D	

10. Actions you take

Do you prefer to:

Marks

Make a new friend	A
Change your approach	B
Have a debate	C
Control a situation	D

A	
B	
C	
D	

11. How would you describe yourself

Marks

Practical	A
Rational	B
Friendly	C
Imaginative	D

A	
B	
C	
D	

12. **How someone who did not like you**
    might describe you   Marks

Rebellious	A	
Weak	B	
Over-cautious	C	
Cold	D	

SCORING

Question Number	LD	CC	PF	PC
1.	A	B	D	C
2.	C	D	A	B
3.	B	A	C	D
4.	D	C	B	A
5.	A	B	D	C
6.	C	D	A	B
7.	B	A	C	D
8.	D	C	B	A
9.	A	B	D	C
10.	C	D	A	B
11.	B	A	C	D
12.	D	C	B	A

TOTALS _____ + _____ + _____ + _____

= 120

Figure 8.2

interpretation

Please look at Figures 8.3 to 8.8, which describe each preference and explain what the initials stand for, and set out some of
the activities, attitudes and approaches associated with each
preference or mode.

Analyse and evaluate	Explore and discover
Resist and stay in control	Accept and help others

Figure 8.3   *The four change preferences*

The first point to make is that, apart from one or two exceptional people, we operate in different modes at different times
when experiencing change. However, we may have a strong
preference for a particular mode, in which case we are likely to
rely on that approach most of the time. Before interpreting the
profile as a whole, let us first look at each mode, as if we were
operating in that mode, and consider what that means in terms
of approach.

logical detached (LD)

In this mode we are unemotional, and have a rational perspective. We will be interested in the facts of the matter, and the
implications; trying to make sense of things. We will not be
challenging the nature and dimensions of the change, or

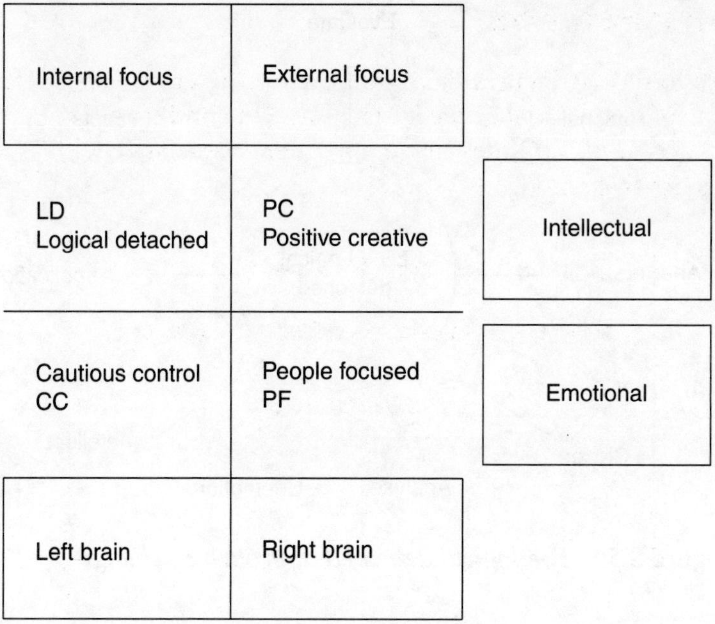

Internal focus	External focus		
LD Logical detached	PC Positive creative	Intellectual	
Cautious control CC	People focused PF	Emotional	
Left brain	Right brain		

Figure 8.4 *Divisions of the brain*

considering the emotional impact on ourselves or others, but focusing on an analysis of the event and what it means.

We shall use the same example in each case, so that the differences can be highlighted. Let us assume that we have been told by the personnel department that there may be a promotion for us from, say, assistant manager in our section to manager. For a logical detached person, the promotion makes obvious sense in career progression terms. We would find out such things as when the promotion was to occur, why we had been selected, what it meant in extra pay and non-financial benefits; we would check up that our understanding of the role and responsibilities was clear, whether there were any rivals for the job, what the selection process and timing would be, what the probability of getting the job would be, and so on – all the logical questions.

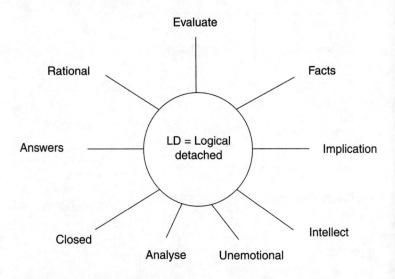

Figure 8.5 *The logical detached approach to change*

If the answers made sense, we would be happy. The LD approach is closed, in the sense that we accept the change for what it is, then ask the questions that resolve the issues arising from the change.

In real life, we would not stay in that mode throughout, particularly when we first learnt about the change, but if we have a very high LD score, and there is a big gap between that and the next score, the chances are we are very logical, emotionally controlled people, and would react in the way suggested.

cautious control (CC)
In this mode our reaction is fundamentally emotional, negative and self-centred. We shall instinctively resist the change, because it necessarily disrupts the status quo, with which we are happy. Depending on the nature of the change we may deny its existence, as can happen with sudden and traumatic changes.

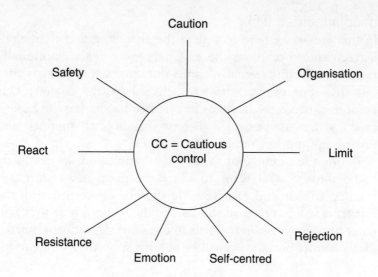

Figure 8.6 *The cautious control approach to change*

We are in a fight to control our environment, under threat from the change. We automatically tend to accentuate the negative, expressing our views logically and, if necessary, illogically. If we fight in vain, and the change is forced upon us, then we try to minimise the damage and maximise the connection to the present and past. So when we hear about the possible promotion, our instant internal reaction is, 'No thanks!' Politically it might not be possible to state that so baldly, so we might demur, mentioning how happy we are in the current role, and how good we are at that job, or we might try to postpone, suggesting the timing is not quite right – a year or so later we would absolutely love promotion – or we might go for the 'I don't feel I am quite ready for it, haven't developed the right skills yet' supplementary approach.

However, if our fight is in vain, and we are promoted, then we have a pragmatic and organised approach so that the new environment can become comfortable as soon as possible.

people focused (PF)

In this mode, we tend to accept the change, rather than challenge, explore or resist the experience; we react emotionally rather than intellectually, and our primary focus is not ourselves but others who are affected by the change. Our emotional needs are likely to be satisfied by sharing the experience as far as possible, thereby gaining us support and providing support to those also affected.

Taking the example of the possible promotion, we are likely to be pleased, and want to share the good news with colleagues, friends and relatives. We shall be concerned with the impact it will have on all the staff in the section, how they will react to our more senior status in the same department, particularly former peers, who will be put in a subordinate role to us.

positive creative (PC)

In this mode we enjoy change, like taking risks, and want to be part of the future that change is creating. We tend not to be

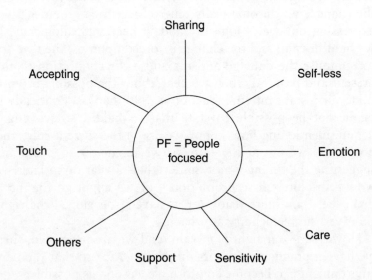

Figure 8.7 *The people focused approach to change*

emotionally involved with the consequences of change on others and ourselves, but are wrapped up in the dynamics of change – full of questions and ideas as we explore the possibilities change brings in its wake.

Considering the possible promotion, we would be interested in making sure we knew what the job entailed; we would be enthusiastic; we would explore the boundaries and constraints, challenge them, consider new approaches (as, in this instance, we would have a good idea of the current job, as it is held by our boss), new ways of meeting the objectives and new objectives to meet.

In real life, if we only used this mode, we probably would not get the job! The likely reaction of a boss (to whom inevitably we would be talking at some stage), whose old job is being given to a subordinate who questions and challenges that boss's approach (which is likely to be the perception of the boss, though not the intention of the subordinate with his or her PC hat on) would be negative.

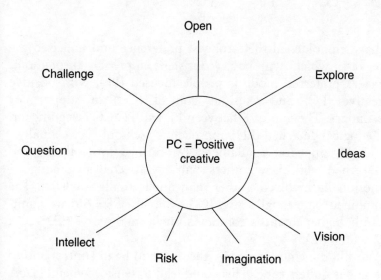

Figure 8.8   *The positive creative approach to change*

the profile

The assessment forced us to choose, and so the profile indicates which mode or modes we prefer. The stronger the preference in relative terms, the more likely are we to adopt the particular mode or modes preferred, when experiencing change.

Additionally, the profile indicates the extent to which we are likely to initiate change. For instance, if we have a score of, say, 36 or more in PC (positive creative) and 24 or less in CC (cautious control), showing that PC is a strong mode and CC a weak mode, then we shall often be initiators of change, whereas with the reverse scoring we shall be maintainers of the status quo.

We now consider two profiles and highlight the key implications. This will help your understanding of the implications behind your own profile. All names have been changed.

Hazel

LD	CC	PF	PC
22	30	**38**	30

I have emboldened the strongest preference and italicised the weakest, which will be a consistent approach throughout. Hazel's preferred mode is people focused (PF), with positive creative (PC) and cautious control (CC) in support or secondary. The gap of 8 between PF and PC/CC is significant. The logical detached (LD) approach is used only occasionally.

Hazel appears fundamentally caring for others and concerned with how others will be affected by change – emotionally involved, rather than intellectually involved. The combined 'emotional' scores (CC + PF; 30 + 38 = 68) are significantly higher than the combined intellectual scores (LD + PC; 22 + 30 = 52).

Within the emotional side, the desire to be in control and to be safe is quite strong. This could lead to tension when Hazel's feelings for others and the exciting creative side conflict with the need to stay in control, keep both feet on the ground and connect to the present and the past.

Within the intellectual side, there is a preference towards the possibilities of change, and excitement with change itself, rather than a detached analysis of the consequences of change. The change that would be most acceptable for Hazel would:

■ be exciting;
■ be connected to the past;
■ ensure that she stays in control;
■ occur with another person.

Hazel would find it tough to change circumstances without support. The high PF score indicates that Hazel could be bullied into change by a strong personality with whom she is emotionally involved.

As regards initiating change, the difference between her PC and CC scores is exactly zero, and, in the absence of the involvement of another person (a shared venture), she is unlikely to be very proactive.

Rodney

LD	CC	PF	PC
30	*15*	37	38

A difference of one or two points between scores is not significant. We see that Rodney has two preferred modes – people focused and positive creative – with logical detached in support. There is a very low cautious control score (the minimum possible is 12).

Rodney is an individual who likes change and will often initiate it (the difference between the PC and CC scores is a very large 23), and is happy to involve others or at least one other (high PF). There is a strong intellectual bias (68 – 52 = 16) combining both the creative and evaluative aspects (LD = 30).

With his very low CC score, he would be able to react well to traumatic events, by being able to give and receive emotional support, through rationalisation and through the strong PC aspect. He would be able to look beyond and around the event, and generate options and approaches outside the limitations and perceived realities, which would blind someone with a high CC score.

However, another aspect of the low CC score is that there may well be occasions when Rodney is controlled by, rather than controlling, change. The low perceived preference for control can result in the absence of control.

how we compare

While it is helpful to look at the absolute scores and the implications of differences and less or more preferred modes, additional value can be gained by comparing us with the norms – combining and averaging the scores of all those who have filled in the assessment. There are two such profiles, as men and women are not identical, on average, for this particular questionnaire.

the female profile

LD	CC	PF	PC
27	28	35	30

We see here LD and CC scores that are nearly balanced, a preference for PF and a moderate PC score. There is a preference for emotional (PF + CC = 63) rather than intellectual responses (LD + PC = 57), a difference of 6. The small difference between CC and PC suggests, on average, that change initiated will be small and connected, rather than discontinuous, with a preference for a partner (high PF).

the male profile

LD	CC	PF	PC	
31	26	30	33	
27	28	35	30	female profile
4	(2)	(5)	3	difference

There is a greater preference for a logically detached approach to change, slightly less resistance, less concern with the impact on others, and greater desire for positive exploration. There is a reversal of the female intellectual/emotional balance, with LD + PC = 64 and PF + CC = 56, a difference of 8. The gap of 7 between PC and CC suggests that men are more the initiators of change than women. This is, of course, on average. There will be many profiles of individuals where there is no gender bias.

playing to strengths

There is always a danger that we shall start feeling dissatisfied with ourselves when we start 'objectively' considering how we approach change, or the conclusions of any questionnaire. This is assuming that we do not react to any feeling of emerging conscious incompetence with the CC response, 'What a load of rubbish. I reject all this nonsense.'

In fact, the higher your CC score, the more likely it is that you have, or are moving into, a rejection mode. If you have a high LD score, you may well be finding flaws in the instrument, where you perceive a logical inconsistency, and starting the rejection process: in other words there may be rejection on both logical and emotional grounds.

Those who have a high LD/CC combination may well not be reading this section at all! This is a pity, because there is neither a right or wrong answer, nor a right or wrong change preference mode.

A key to creating growth from change is to develop an integrated approach, using all the responses, as each is needed at different times and phases. This is particularly difficult when we are reacting to change, and is much easier when we initiate change. I want to conclude this section and the book by highlighting the strengths of each approach.

logical detached (LD)

The ability to stand back, be objective, and analyse and evaluate the implications of change is essential to gaining growth. Imposing the necessary discipline of facts and information, and curbing an excess of the improbable, are vital components.

cautious control (CC)

There are considerable strengths in this preference. Change is more acceptable, generally, if it is delivered in stages and is strongly connected to the past. The Japanese, who are a very conservative nation, have used this preference very well in the past in developing continuous improvement cultures. Paradoxically, we could argue that the CC preference is now culturally too low, and is vital in obtaining continuous improvement cultures. Provided the strong CC individual recognises the need for improvement rather than radical change, he or she will be very useful in both making and selling the connections to the status quo.

people focused (PF)

Change almost invariably involves others as well as ourselves. The abilities to recognise how others are affected, to listen to and understand their concerns, and to support them through change, smooth the path for all of us.

positive creative (PC)

Change is never set in concrete. A creative, exploring and challenging approach to change can significantly improve both its nature and the outcomes.

references and further reading

Bandler, R and Grinder, J (1979) *Frogs Into Princes*, Real People Press, Moab, UT

Bennis, W (1989) *On Becoming a Leader*, Addison-Wesley, Boston, MA

Blanchard, K and Johnson, S (1983) *The One Minute Manager*, Fontana, London

Covey, S (1989) *The Seven Habits of Highly Effective People*, Simon and Schuster, London

Drucker, P (1967) *The Effective Executive*, Heinemann Professional Publishing, London

Eales-White, R (1992) *The Power of Persuasion: Improving your performance and leadership skills*, Kogan Page, London

Eales-White, R (1996) *How to be a Better Team-Builder*, Kogan Page, London

Gallwey, T (1975) *The Inner Game of Golf*, Jonathan Cape, London

Harrison, R (1991) *Humanising Change: A culture-based approach*, Harrison Associates, USA

Katzenback, J (1998) *Teams at the Top*, Harvard Business School Press, Cambridge, MA

Kelley, R (1988) In praise of followers, *Harvard Business Review*, 88606 (Nov-Dec)

Margerison, C and McCann, D (1991) *Team Management Systems: The linking skills manual*, TMS (UK)

Minto, B (1987) *The Pyramid Principle: Logic in writing and thinking*, Pitman, London

Montebello, A and Buzzotta, V (1993) Work teams that work, *Training and Development* 47(3) pp 59–64

Moss Kanter, R (1983) *The Change Masters: Corporate entrepreneurs at work*, Simon and Schuster, New York

Peters, T (1992) *Liberation Management*, Knopf, New York

Romiszowski, A (1984) *Producing Instructional Systems*, Kogan Page, London

Van Maurik, J (1996) *The Portable Leader*, McGraw-Hill, Maidenhead

Van Maurik J (2001) *Writers on Leadership*, Penguin, London

Whitmore, J (1992) *Coaching for Performance: A practical guide to growing your skills*, Brealey, London